The Revd Ronni Lamont worked for many years as a teacher and spent 16 years in parish ministry, most recently at St John the Evangelist in Bexley. She has a wealth of training and development experience, and specializes in creativity and innovation, children's spirituality and pastoral training (see <www.creative-spirituality.org.uk>). The editor of <www.assemblies.org.uk>, she is the author of the widely acclaimed *Understanding Children Understanding God*, also published by SPCK (2007).

THE GOD WHO LEADS US ON

Story Meditations on Salvation

Ronni Lamont

First published in Great Britain in 2008

Society for Promoting Christian Knowledge
36 Causton Street
London SW1P 4ST

British Library Cataloguing-in-Publication Data
A catalogue record for this book is available from the British Library

ISBN 978–0–281–06076–4

1 3 5 7 9 10 8 6 4 2

Typeset by Graphicraft Ltd., Hong Kong
Printed in Great Britain by Ashford Colour Press

Contents

This book is dedicated to the people of St John the Evangelist, Bexley, who heard the stories and encouraged me to tell more.

Introduction

A man that looks on glass
On it may stay his eye;
Or if he pleases, through it pass
And then the heavens espy.
George Herbert

I remember reading these words at school and wondering what on earth they were about: it's the third verse of Herbert's wonderful hymn 'Teach me, my God and King'. There was a footnote in the hymn book explaining that the 'famous stone' to which the last verse alludes was the philosopher's stone and what that was. Of course, to a post-Harry Potter generation that allusion needs no explanation, whereas the verse above required some thought on the part of the 11-year-old me.

It refers to the fact that in the seventeenth century, when Herbert penned the lines, glass was not as it is today. It would not be smooth and shiningly transparent, but the sort of glass we see in heritage properties – wobbly and slightly coloured. A bit like the stained-glass windows in the church opposite my study window. And it is possible for one's eye to stay on the glass, to admire and look at the picture; but the glass is designed to take us beyond what it represents, to the story shown in the picture that the artist stained the glass to represent.

Many sermons stop at that top level – what the words actually say, with some contextual background, and then a conclusion about 'what this has to say for us today'. That's fine for many Sundays, but in my ministry I began to struggle with the big festivals; what can I say about Christmas/Easter that's new? That will give folks something to chew over along with the turkey?

So I began to rewrite scripture, from a new point of view; to imagine the sights and the sounds and to recreate the scene for today's listeners. To transport people back so that they could imagine that they were there, witnessing the events of scripture.

These story sermons proved immensely popular, and so are offered to you. They were written to be read aloud, so you may choose to do that. If you use this book in the context of a group, share them aloud and give time to contemplate the images that you see, the insights that you have gained.

Most of all, give them time to sink into your being, which may involve more than one reading. Take them with you through the day, and reflect on what they are saying to you. We are far removed from the heroes and heroines whose stories you are about to encounter; let them speak across the ages of time, and so may you be strengthened in your own journey as you travel with them, and the God who leads us on.

1

The mark of Cain

Genesis 3—4

I never knew it would end like this. I never dreamt it would end like this. How could I? Who could have seen this coming? Who could have predicted this end?

It all began so well; Adam and me, in the garden. Ha! How naive we were in those days – before the fruit, the fruit of the tree in the centre of the garden. The luscious, sweet fruit that spelled the beginning of the end for us – we thought.

I don't remember being small. Maybe that's because I wasn't. Because Adam, he and I, we were made like this – adults, fully formed. No mother, no father, except for . . .

Adam tells me he was first – the first around here, the first in the garden, the first to know Yahweh, the Creator. He tells me that he was here, and the animals were here, and the birds, and the fish, even the ants, but I wasn't. He tells me that he went to sleep one day, and when he woke up, there I was. Like a rabbit out of a hat, as one of your so-called magicians might say.

No, I'm not joking. Adam says he went to sleep, and when he woke up, Yahweh gave me to him. Why? To be his companion. To be his partner. To be the mother of his children. Because Adam knew that he was different from the animals. That we were different. That we knew Yahweh, and that somehow Yahweh knew us in a different way from how he knew the animals.

It was lovely at first. We lived in the garden, with the animals and plants, eating what we needed, picking fruit, drinking the water from the stream. I've never tasted fruit or water so good, ever since . . .

But I found myself wondering how long it could go on. The same days. The same nights. The stars and the moon by night, the sun by day, Yahweh walking in the garden with us in the evening. How foolish I was – why couldn't I be happy with paradise?

And I found myself looking at that fruit.

The fruit we ate, that we were allowed to eat, was wonderful – full of juice and flavour. But you know how it is – the one we were forbidden smelled so good – looked so good. So when the serpent told me that it wasn't poison, that it wouldn't kill me; what would *you* have done? Would *you* have been able to resist?

I'm sure now that if I'd had more to do, to occupy me, I wouldn't have stood there, day by day, looking at that tree, that particular tree, and the fruit that grew upon it.

And then, as I said, there was that serpent.

We got along fine, me and the serpent. It did its thing, we did ours. So we only met from time to time. But I began to notice that when I was there, at the special tree, so was the serpent.

You know the rest, don't you?

I ate. Adam ate. Yahweh threw us out.

Yahweh wasn't joking about bringing forth children in pain. First Cain, and then Abel. And all their lives, they were jealous of each other and for my love. I tried so hard to love them both the same – and in the end I did, but differently. As differently as they were different.

And years later, here we are. Cain has come home with blood on his hands, and darkness in his heart. And on his face, there's a mark. He said he tried to wash it off, but Yahweh made the mark. Yahweh marked him out as special – the mark is a warning and a sign.

My heart is broken once again. Abel, my gentle-hearted boy, is gone. Cain is going – going to the land of Nod to find a wife and try to forget us, and what he did.

But Yahweh has promised that no matter where Cain goes, Yahweh will never forget him.

Now I know we can never go back. Yahweh, what did we do?

Yahweh, what did we do?

Reflection

Think of the 'big regrets' in your life: how far are you thinking back?

Have you ever given these regrets to God, and left them with God?

Could you do that, and walk away, leaving them in God's hands? If not – why do you want to hang on to these regrets?

Perhaps today you could leave them behind, and walk into this new season with less baggage.

Prayer

Lord, help me to leave my baggage at your feet,
to walk away from it
and really leave it with you.
Amen.

2

Abram's call

Genesis 15.1–12, 17–18

There's an old saying we have among ourselves: God, if this is how you treat your friends, no wonder you have so few.

That's about right, too. My life with God – I could write pages, you'd be bored, but my life with God, it's been weird.

Long time ago now, I lived in a city. Not like this one that you live in, but an ancient, beautiful city of tall buildings, great squares, where the merchants sell their wares, children play and adults sit and drink and talk. Ur, city of my dreams. City of my youth and childhood, where I married Sarai, where it all began.

I have always known God. Some people, they're like that. Still you meet them. And he always knew me. So, when one day he tells me to move out of the city, to follow his call, with all my people, animals and slaves, well, that's what we did. Sarai, she didn't like it, because she doesn't hear God; she has to trust me. And she thought I'd had too much to drink.

'Sarai,' I said, 'it *is* him, and he is calling to us from the desert. That is where we need to go.'

And that is where we went, with Lot, my nephew, who has no one else to care for him and to find him a wife.

We went to Bethel, and then to Mamre, but there was no food, so we travelled down to Egypt.

What trouble I made there. Sarai is beautiful, and so I pretended she was my sister. So Pharaoh, he takes her and pops my Sarai into his harem. Who can blame him? But then plagues come sweeping down upon Pharaoh and his house. I confessed, and Pharaoh, he let us all go – no punishment, no trouble, off we all went. And so did the plagues, until many years later, but that's someone else's story.

Then Lot got himself captured in some minor skirmish along the border and I had to rescue him. I keep thinking, I'm getting older, but life keeps happening to me and mine; we go from place to place, and find ourselves at Bethel, again, so we returned to Mamre, to the Oaks. How I loved it there – and so did Sarai. A strange place. A place where God was nearby.

It was shortly after we'd returned that I had the dream.

Sarai had been tearful again, because we have no children. Pharaoh had many down in Egypt, but Sarai, she bore him none. Likewise me; we have no children, yet the good Lord, he keeps telling me that this land is for me and mine. Lot's well in here, I think. For Lot is all we have.

Sarai, she'd been crying. Another month gone by, another chance dashed. So I left the tents, and wandered into the desert. I must have slept there, for in my sleep he came to me, just as before.

Ishmael, my slave girl's son, he is not to be my issue, but, he said, Sarai is to have descendants like the stars in the sky.

You don't see stars any more, not like I did. Stars that covered the night sky, glorious light in the black of the eastern night sky.

The stars I have seen have no number. They are endless, like sand on the shore of the sea.

So the Lord told me, so my descendants were to be. I wondered just how we were supposed to manage this, but the Lord, he's telling me it will be so. I don't argue with the good Lord.

I sacrificed to the Lord, as I have been taught; a heifer, a goat, a dove and a pigeon. And then the dark came. I am used to darkness, but this was like the inside of the night. I could see nothing, and the stars, they went out. Gently they vanished into the pitch black surrounding me. I was terrified. I felt the darkness enter my soul, leaving me empty and alone. Never have I felt such fear, such unworthiness.

Then I saw; a smoking fire pot and a flaming torch. What these were I do not know, but still I see them and still I think on them.

And again, the voice of the Lord.

I give you, and your descendants, this land. All of it.

Again he speaks of descendants. Again he gives me the land. I shall treasure this place. I shall care for the land. And I await the Lord's promise to be fulfilled – that one day my descendants shall number as the stars in heaven.

The Lord, he keeps his promises. But sometimes he takes a long time.

Reflection

How does God keep his promises in your life?

Think about the areas of your life that you've kept from God, possibly without intending to . . .

God has promised us so much, but how do we respond?

The Lord, he keeps his promises, but sometimes he takes a long time.

Reflect on the things that you are still waiting for from God, but know are on their way, and thank God for all the things you already have.

3

A son for Sarai

Genesis 18.1–15

Me 'n' Abram – sorry, Abraham – we go back a long, long time. Been married for about 60 years, I reckon, and he knew me when I was just a child. He used to come to my family's house, back in Ur, and drink with my elder brother. My parents knew his family, so when he asked for me, no one was surprised, just pleased to be rid of me with such a small dowry! Thirty camels is not to be sniffed at, but my family had hundreds of the things, all working across the desert, carrying all the things that people want; the little luxuries that come from lands far off that women use to put each other down; you know the sort of thing I mean.

And I was Abram's first wife. And only wife, much to everyone's – and my – amazement. Always said I was all he wanted – apart from a son, of course.

And a son was the one thing we couldn't have. Or a daughter either, but that wasn't quite the same. I bore my grief; Abram, he just sort of pined, but he wouldn't take another woman, even when I suggested it. The shame: I can't speak of it, it was so bad.

I have to confess to being more than a little shocked when he came in one day and announced that we were moving. Moving – and him 75 years old. And to where, I asked him? And he didn't know! Had some sort of religious experience on the roof, comes down and says, pack up, Sarai, we're on the move.

Now, that's fine for the nomads. Beautiful tents and stuff they have – you'd hardly know they were on the move; but where do we get these tents, I ask?

Seems like he's got it all sorted. Got a bargain – wouldn't you just bet on it – and it's time to pack the camels, gather the herds and the people and go. Where? Into the desert.

Maybe this is how he works out the grief of childlessness. Maybe I upset him, I know I'm a bit house-proud, but wouldn't you have been?

Well, it was no use arguing. We've been married for long enough for me to know that set of his shoulders. We're going, and that's it.

So, off we went. Weeks, we were, wandering under the sun, pitching the tent for a couple of days to give the sheep a chance, and then off again.

We came eventually to the plain. It was beautiful. I've never seen so much lush pasture. Lot's eyes grew round – he was always after the easy life. 'I'll take here,' he said, laughing. Abram and me, we went on, leaving Lot and his family looking like the cat that got the cream. We went on, to Hebron and then on again, a couple of miles, to the sanctuary at Mamre.

Is it the trees, or just history, that makes it such a holy place? They say there's been an altar here for as long as people have been in the land. That special feeling of heaven coming down, and earth rising up? You've been there too?

So we pitched the tent, set the sheep grazing and loosed the camels. All was peaceful for a couple of days. We found grain to grind, bread to cook, fruit to gather. It was a good place.

Abram – sorry, Abraham – has a silly habit of sitting out in the midday sun. After all these years, you'd think he'd know better, but he still does it. Sitting out, at the door to the tent, thinking, when there they are – three men, like they'd grown up out of the ground. Me, I skidaddle into the tent, where I should be, and start to make bread. It's hospitality time.

Abraham goes up and greets the visitors – they'll have to stay with us until evening, or roast out in this sun. So they agree to stay. And I can hear in his voice that there's something about them making him uneasy. Not that they look shifty – rather the opposite – they just look a bit disconnected, if you get my drift.

Abraham goes and kills a goat kid, and we roast it with the herbs that grow roundabouts. They do what visitors do, and come back looking refreshed and ready to eat. So they do.

And then they ask after me. Where is Sarah? they ask – not even my old name, Sarai, but Sarah.

Abraham, he almost chokes on his bit of goat – and it wasn't tough – Sarah, he exclaims, why, she's in the tent.

'When I come back in a year, she will have a child,' one of them says.

Me! A child? I'm way past my sell-by date, I scream in my head. And besides – not wishing to be crude – it takes two to make a baby, and Abraham's showing his age as well! I must have laughed out loud, to try to kill the pain. And they heard me.

Abraham calls me out. I could have killed him. Imagine what a fool I felt. 'Why did you laugh?'

Why did I laugh? Couldn't he see why I laughed?

But the man stuck to his word – 'You will have a child.' And when I looked at him, I wasn't going to argue. He believed it, even if I couldn't.

And then they left, the three of them, down towards Sodom. I was so worried about them going down there that I sent Abraham to warn them about the place. But that's another story.

But, do you know, here I am, enormous with child. And I just know that it's a boy.

When we talk about those men, Abraham, he goes quiet. When I asked him who they were, he went quiet. Don't you know? he asked. Didn't you feel who they were? That was the Lord, and his angels.

So, there you go. No wonder I felt uncomfortable. No wonder they looked strange. But would I recognize them again? Not by their faces, but I would recognize that strange feeling inside. Don't they say that many have entertained angels unawares? Well, that's me. Totally unaware. How about you?

Reflection

'Do not neglect to show hospitality to strangers, for by doing that some have entertained angels without knowing it' (Hebrews 13.2).

Our tradition of hospitality is somewhat lacking compared to that of Abraham's era. How can we make people welcome today – in our homes, in our workplaces and in our churches?

Prayer

Lord, grant me the gift of hospitality,
that I too may entertain angels without knowing it.
Amen.

4

A wife for Isaac

Genesis 24

Here you are then: Eliezer, the oldest of Abraham's servants. You've travelled miles and miles and miles, back to the country near Haran, from where, years and years before, Abraham and all his household had set off for the land that the Lord God had promised to Abraham. He had been merely 80 or so, his wife Sarah, well, one didn't enquire. No Isaac; years of travel and a visit by angels had led to Isaac. The fuss and bother of Hagar and Ishmael, the years of waiting and watching. And now, Sarah was dead and Abraham not long for this world either. He has bidden you to return to Haran, to find a wife for Isaac: someone to carry on the line, to be the mother of Israel, and not from among the Canaanites; and under no circumstances is Isaac to go back to Haran himself.

What do you do? It seems like a wild goose chase; why should some poor female travel out into the back of beyond and further, with the name of a long-gone relation all that you have?

You're sitting by a well. It's really quite scenic – the troughs at the top for the animals, the steps cut into the side of the cliff to go down to the spring, the water there at the bottom. Your camels are at the top, but you have no pitcher to descend to the water; and besides, it's woman's work, that.

How will you know the one? How will you tell which one the Lord has picked out for Isaac, if any? How will you find her, and her family, and then tell them the news?

Then you see a woman approaching, with her friends. Pitchers on their shoulders, they walk, glide towards you. Help me, Lord, to know who she is . . .

You notice one rather than the others. Why her? Well, you just do. Something about the grace of her walk, her carriage, her personality shining in her steady eyes.

Here goes . . .

'Would you fetch me a drink? I don't have a bowl to fetch water.'

'Certainly,' she replies, demurely avoiding your eyes. 'For you and your camels.'

So off she goes, down the steps, fills the pitcher and empties it into the trough. Back down the steps, fetches the water, and into the trough . . . how many times, many times. And she gives you water to drink as well. Sweet water, the way it is after a desert journey.

Thank you, Lord.

So you ask her who she is, and she tells you, and invites you to her home for the night – to share hospitality and hear the news from far away.

So, Lord, she's the one.

Yes, Eliezer, she's the one.

Prayer

Lord, sometimes you ask me to do things that seem daft, foolhardy, impossible.
Help me to know that you will be there with me, accompanying me every step of the way, holding my hand and speaking in my ear.
Give me the confidence to step out in faith when I hear your call, to do your will.
Amen.

5

Jacob's ladder

Genesis 28.10–19a

Look at this place – full of stalls and beggars. There's the altar, the priest and the people, all expecting their miracle, their special experience. It was a bit different then. My gosh it was different.

I was running, running for my life. My elder brother Esau, Esau the hunter, Esau my father's favourite, he'd sold me his birthright for a bowl of lentil soup. Talk about getting to a man through the stomach! But he was always the same; if he was hungry, he was starving . . . Give me some of that, he said. Certainly . . . what will you pay? I replied. Me, the cunning younger brother that I'd always been. Always looking to assert my brain over his brawn. So he sold it to me.

Then my mother, Rebecca, always on my side, suggested we tricked my half-blind father, Isaac, and so I got the blessing too . . . no wonder Esau was angry. No wonder he threatened to kill me.

So I ran. Ran for my life, back to Rebecca's home, to her brother, Laban.

I got here about nightfall on the first day. My head was spinning. I was terrified of what Esau might do, how he might track me and hunt me down, as I'd seen him do with wolves, deer and other animals.

I came here. But here was nowhere in particular. Just a clearing, high up, where I lay down to sleep.

I found a flat stone to use as a pillow, and watched the stars, as I slipped into sleep.

But what a dream I had.

I dreamed I saw a stairway, a stairway into heaven. Not a ladder, but a ramp, with angels going up and down, and at the top was the very doorway between earth and heaven. Behind the doorway was a light – and the light came down, and stood next to me.

I am the Lord, I heard, as I lay paralysed with fear and awe.

And the Lord promised to be with me, to bless me and my family, and that he would bring me back, back home, eventually.

So I woke up. The place was just like any other clearing in the scrub, but I knew the Lord was there.

So, I built an altar, and named the clearing Beth-El – the Lord is here.

Here we are today, with thousands of pilgrims looking for the Lord. But *he* finds *you*; and he's not here any more than he's anywhere else. Whatever else I took from that dream, it was that the Lord is with me. Beth-El is wherever I am. I just have to remember that the Lord is here. Always.

Reflection

Pause and think about that last sentence: Beth-El is wherever I am. I just have to remember the Lord is here. Always.

Reflect that the Lord is with you, now, wherever you are.

How easy do you find it to remember God's presence?

Take a moment of quiet to thank God for his continuing love in your life, and for God's love for you, here and now.

Prayer

Lord God, help me to remember that you are with me today,
No matter where I go,
No matter how I feel.
May your love blossom up within me, and spread to all those with whom I share time today.
Amen.

6

The parting of the Red Sea

Exodus 14.21–31

I don't know what to say to you, mate; I know just what you mean. What on earth is going on? I know the big man keeps saying that the Lord is with us, but I ask you – how do we know? I know there was all that shenanigans in Egypt before we got out, but what about now? What's going on now? Has he brought us here to die, to drown, when Pharaoh's chariots come up over the sand dunes and drive us all before them into the sea?

You say you don't know about what's been going on? Where've you been? Wrong side of the Nile, clearly. Well, sit you down, sir, and I'll tell you the story so far – the story of how that man seems to have taken an entire nation in, and brought us here, out in the wilderness and to the brink of disaster.

I suppose it all began with Joseph and his family. They came down into Egypt many years ago – hundreds of years ago – supposedly because there was a famine in their land. Their land is supposed to be on the other side of this wilderness, but I don't know anyone who's been there lately.

Well, they came to Egypt many years ago, and settled down. Joseph somehow made himself indispensable to the Pharaoh, and the family had it made, there in the royal palace. But the family grew, and eventually became too big for comfort, so later on another Pharaoh decided that here was a potential army – of slaves! Overnight, wealthy, comfortable people found themselves evicted to the land of Goshen and forced into slavery. I know we make a good brick – but that's only been for the last few generations.

So, fast forward and you get to you 'n' me, working our socks off and being beaten for it. Male children started being slaughtered, and at that point we began to mutter even more under our breath. The claim is that the big man – he's one of us – was somehow smuggled into the royal palace as a baby, and Pharaoh's daughter took pity on him and brought him up as her own. He vanished after a sudden death in the palace, vanished for years; but then he was back and challenging the Pharaoh to let us go!

You've got to be joking! As if Pharaoh's going to let his workforce leave for nothing – who's going to finish that tomb of his out in the desert if we're not around? Who's going to repair the palace, to build houses up next time the earth moves? No – Pharaoh laughed in his face, they say.

But he returned. And threatened Pharaoh – said our God would smite the Egyptians. Pharaoh laughed again: who was big enough to smite the Egyptians? But strange things began to happen in the land of Egypt: first the river turned to blood – the fish all died, and the smell! But no – he wouldn't let the slaves go. The next thing that happened was a plague of frogs – everywhere! You couldn't move for the things! Eventually they died off – but still he wouldn't let us go! Then there was a plague of gnats – urgh! Then flies – even more urgh! Then there was a pestilence, and all the animals died – more flies. Then everyone got boils, and then there were storms – terrible storms. You'd think he'd have got the message by now, but no, he wouldn't let us go. After the storms came locusts, and then the sky was dark for three whole days. Everyone was terrified – we thought the end had come. But the sun returned, and Pharaoh said no again.

Then, and I shudder to think of it, then came the deaths. We had been told to hold a feast one day – to slaughter young lambs and mark our doorposts with their blood. Then we put on our outer clothes, as if we were about to run, and ate the roast meat. The next morning we woke to the sound of a city in mourning. Women wailing – then that awful silence when the women were worn out. The first-born child of every family had died – except for ours. The blood on the door, the big man said, the blood on the door saved our children.

Pharaoh let us go then. We walked out of that land with our heads held high. But that was just a couple of days ago. With so many of us, and all our animals, it takes for ever to cover the ground. And here we are – at this sea. How can we get to the Promised Land now? Pharaoh's sending his chariots – look! You can see the clouds of dust! And we're trapped. What's the big man's God going to do now to save us? Dry up the sea so that we can just march over on the sea bed?

Pass my scarf, would you – it's that one, there. There's a terrible wind getting up.

Reflection

God works in mysterious ways.

Think back over your life. Has God done amazing things for you, but in a way where it was only when you looked back that you saw the pattern? If so, give thanks, and spend some time remembering the way that God has been active in your life.

If you don't see God active in your life, spend a few moments asking God to reveal to you where he has indeed been at work.

7

Naomi's story

The book of Ruth

My life, my life: where to begin. Such a long life; and at times, I wished to not be alive any more. The hurt, the pain, and the joys that I can tell you! The places I have seen, the people, the children; ah yes, I have had a long life. And it was only dull at the beginning!

When I was of age, my parents married me to Elimelech, and I bore him two sons, Mahlon and Chilion. How I loved those boys! They knew the country around Bethlehem better than I know the lines on my face, and they loved each other! But hard times came, and Elimelech decided we should move on, to the land of Moab, where there was food and water. So we did, and for a while, there was indeed food and water. And there were young women, and my boys became young men, and they both married local girls, Orpah and Ruth. So for a while, life was good. The sun shone on my life and I was happy. But then the fever came, and took not just my husband, but also my sons, leaving me and the two girls all widows. What could we do? It was either starve or each of us go back whence we had come, so we said our farewells and the girls went to go home. But Ruth wouldn't go. She came with me to the border country, where she burst into tears and refused to leave me! What could I do? I had nothing. No boys that she could marry. No money to buy food, just distant kin from whom I could claim shelter and support, of a kind. But for Ruth there was nothing.

But she would not go. She claimed she wanted to live with me, and die with me. And for all I knew, the dying was the more likely of the two. But we said goodbye to Orpah and to Moab, and travelled back, to Bethlehem.

It was harvest when we arrived. All the town seemed to be in uproar at my story – but talk is cheap. When we came to nightfall, we slept in a barn.

There was a kinsman, we learned, and he was rich. Boaz had done well, and I remembered the chubby baby of my cousin as she'd bounced him on her knee. He was the first-born son, spoilt but happy. Now he was a man, and single too.

So I sent Ruth to glean in his fields, where we had rights. She did, and she did well. That night we ate and felt full; the first time for weeks.

The next day, she went again, and people were told to give her the best gleanings. Boaz had noticed her – as he should, for Ruth is a beauty, and not from round here. That night I told her what she had to do to claim family rights.

So she went, and when he was asleep, she lay at his feet. He claimed to be shocked when he woke to find her there, but Ruth said he's a rotten liar. She remained there all night.

So it was that with time, Boaz married my Ruth. Joy came to my life again, as they had a son, Obed. Obed was like my own son; Ruth let me nurse him, and I was like a mother to him. Ruth bore Boaz other sons, and the household grew even richer.

With time Obed and then his son Jesse, grew up, both the image of Boaz; and Jesse's eye was caught by a local girl. They married and their family was healthy and strong – eight sons – and I was still able to dandle the youngest, David, when he was born. The most beautiful baby that Bethlehem has ever seen, I declare.

Yes, what a life, full of twists and turns. You say that the Lord watches over us all, and I wonder why? Why the pain, the journeying, the hunger and the grief? Why couldn't we have been just a normal family, with grandchildren through the first marriages and land of our own?

I did ask Boaz once, what he thought. He just looked at Ruth in that doe-eyed manner of his and smiled. Me, I just look at David and smile. My David, my little shepherd boy. May life be kinder to you, my love. May life be kinder to you.

Prayer

Lord God,
God of heaven and earth,
Of Jews and Christians,
Help me to hold on to my faith when life is hard
And to give thanks to you when life is good.
Amen.

8

Jeremiah's call

Jeremiah 1.4–10

The word of the LORD came to me saying,

> 'Before I formed you in the womb I knew you,
> and before you were born I consecrated you;
> I appointed you a prophet to the nations.'

Then I said, 'Ah, Lord GOD! Truly I do not know how to speak, for I am only a boy.' But the LORD said to me,

> 'Do not say, "I am only a boy";
> for you shall go to all to whom I send you,
> and you shall speak whatever I command you,
> Do not be afraid of them,
> for I am with you to deliver you,
> says the LORD.'

Then the LORD put out his hand and touched my mouth; and the LORD said to me,

> 'Now I have put my words in your mouth.
> See, today I appoint you over nations and over kingdoms,
> to pluck up and to pull down,
> to destroy and to overthrow,
> to build and to plant.'

What do you do? I'm a regular guy, work as a priest in the sanctuary, come from Ananoth in Benjamin. So I'm in the sanctuary one day, and I'm convinced I can hear the voice speaking to me, again. All through my life it's come and gone, since I can first remember. This overpowering sense of the almighty, or Yahweh, then that quiet voice in my head.

I've tried to argue. I'm only young; you can see that. I can't speak well; you can hear that. I'm useless at the proclamations – never been taught how to orate or address a crowd. I've none of the wisdom that comes through the years. Who would respect me as understanding the ways of Yahweh?

But I've also got commitments. I'm betrothed for a start, want to settle down, continue the family line, have children and care for my parents as they grow old. But still the voice comes.

I wouldn't mind if it was telling me good news. Hey, Jeremiah! Go to the king and tell him that it's OK. The kings of Assyria will fall, as will the Pharaoh in Egypt. You won't have to keep indulging in this political roulette that you've developed: Yes, Pharaoh, no, your majesty. Here's this year's tribute, your majesty. Not enough? Well, keep the horses that brought it to Babylon. Oh, Pharaoh, you want more too? Keep the camels, I've got plenty . . .'

No, the voice is telling me that destruction will come first, and the rebuilding is beyond my lifetime. So I've got to go to the king, who's surrounded himself with so-called prophets, who are either tuning into a different Yahweh or telling the king what he *wants* to hear rather than what he *needs* to hear.

I've got to tell him that we are doomed; that the Assyrians are going to destroy everything that we hold dear, that Judah will fall. Yahweh will no longer protect us from the nation states that we lie between. The lion of Assyria has woken and will soon be on the march . . .

And the voice won't go away. It mimics the liturgy that we've used for so long to support and commission those who we think Yahweh is calling. It uses the words that I've heard used over other prophets during my time at the temple . . . I hear the voice, day in, day out. Jeremiah, Jeremiah . . .

And then I had the dream. It was like I've heard others tell of; the hand that came to my mouth, that put something in my mouth. Something so bitter I woke up retching. But it became something so sweet that I never wanted it to leave me – I didn't want to chew it up and swallow it; I wanted to roll my tongue around it, savour the flavour and keep it there for ever.

And the voice told me that this thing in my mouth, it was the word of Yahweh, the word of the Lord.

Now I have put my words in your mouth.
See, today I appoint you over nations and over kingdoms,
to pluck up and to pull down,
to destroy and to overthrow,
to build and to plant.

Who am I, Lord, to say these things? I am only a youth.
I'm scared, I'm alone. Who am I to receive your call?

Do not be afraid of them,
for I am with you to deliver you,
says the LORD.

Reflection

Think about the difficult things that God asks you to do today.

Now reflect for a few minutes on God's words to Jeremiah at the beginning of the chapter.

Take comfort in the words at the end of the story:

Do not be afraid of them,
for I am with you to deliver you,
says the LORD.

9

Psalm 137: 'By the rivers of Babylon'

Greetings, stranger. You like my singing? You say that you too know these words – from your future time, when all the world will hear my song? Ah, the Almighty and his sense of humour! When I wrote those words, the whole of Babylon, the great city, they too were singing my song.

Ah, the poignancy of those lyrics, the haunting melody of the music; this is a perfect psalm, they said. Little did they know that the Jews had another verse – a verse expressing our hatred for these people, these people who destroyed our beloved Zion, and carried us away to their strange, heathen city on the great river Tigris.

I was born in Zion – did you know that? Apparently I have an accent – the best accent to have in all the world, that of the city that the Almighty placed on a high hill, so all the world would come and worship there.

And so they did, for a while. But then they came to take us over – it seemed our little country was the land of milk and honey for Nebuchadnezzar too.

The prophets warned us – for longer than anyone could remember, the prophets came and told us to repent. They told us that the Lord would punish us if we didn't repent and mend our ways. Powerful words stay in my heart:

What does the LORD require of you
but to do justice, and to love kindness,
and to walk humbly with your God?
(Micah 6.8)

But we didn't – we carried on cheating and swindling, especially the poor.

Jeremiah told us – in such dramatic ways – that our end was in sight, but the king refused to listen. First Jehoiakim, then Zedekiah; they wouldn't listen.

So it came. As we knew it would – an army covered the plains before Jerusalem. An army the like of which we had never seen before. You tell me that you have buildings called museums where you can look at pictures and carvings from that time:* men in chariots, men on horses, men on foot. Archers, swordsmen, foot soldiers. The land had vanished under their camp.

And they sat there until we starved. No food could enter Zion. Eventually we came out, on our knees, and Nebuchadnezzar, that wily beast, marched us off to Babylon. Not all of us – just the useful people.

He killed everyone in my family apart from myself. I was the court musician, and he saw that he could take me and let me ply my trade in Babylon. But my wife and children starved. My parents starved and my brother died in the battle.

And I was alive, and in Babylon. I joined the Jewish group there – we tried to keep to ourselves. Rabbis came and taught us and we tried to return to our ways of life. And I wrote songs, songs that you tell me have lived down through the centuries.

And the one you know so well – did you ever read it all in the holy book you have there? Did you ever read the last verses? Those are the ones that we kept for ourselves, and when the captors had left us, those are the words that we sang, to keep our hearts strong, to keep our heads high. Nebuchadnezzar – pah! I spit in his name.

Together, we are strong. Together, we will return to Zion. We will return, and we will rebuild the beautiful city upon the hill, to worship the Almighty once more.

If I forget you, O Jerusalem,
let my right hand wither!
Let my tongue cling to the roof of my mouth,
if I do not remember you.
(Psalm 137.5–6)

Ah Jerusalem, Jerusalem, I will remember you.

---

* The British Museum has a whole gallery dedicated to this period of Babylonian and Assyrian relics.

Reflection

Think back over the hard times that you have gone through in the course of your life. Did God feel close to you at those times, or was God distant?

How do our feelings get in the way of our day-to-day experience of life as Christians?

Do you have any techniques to help you through days when you feel God is distant?

If you don't, take some time to consider what you can do to keep your walk with God positive, and how you handle the more trying days.

10

Malachi reflects

Malachi 4.1–2a

Lord, how long do we have to wait for your servant to reappear? Elijah, the great prophet? You have told me, so many times now, that the day is coming, that the day is soon, when Elijah will reappear and set us right once more.

It's been going on so long, Lord. Yes, we all came back from Babylon, singing as we came, the joy, the happiness – the wine and the sore heads! We came back – the redeemed of the Lord returned to Zion, singing, as Isaiah described. But look what happened.

Did we really not realize that rebuilding a city is hard work? That it never ends?

We came to the ruins, the rubble of Solomon's temple, and began. Lord, that was 40 years ago. We have been rebuilding Jerusalem for ever, it seems, and still there is more rubble, more to be replaced or rebuilt. Your servant, the governor, Nehemiah, he inspires us to work on; but, Lord, how long?

We came back to our land, the land of milk and honey, and we expected that milk and honey to flow. Hah! We had to catch the bees, Lord, and rebuild the hives, before we had any honey; and we had to wait for the calves to grow up and produce their own calves before we had any milk. Some land of milk and honey this turned out to be.

We came back expecting riches, wealth, a life of ease, and we found this mess. No wonder the worship has been so – well, so tatty. People thought it was going to be easy, that you would feel closer here than you did in Babylon – after all, Lord, how could we sing your song in a strange land? But we came back here, and discovered that Israel had become a strange land too. We spoke like Babylonians, dressed like Babylonians, had picked up their habits and lifestyles . . . Israel was no longer the beautiful place that we remembered, not by the time the invading Babylonians and Assyrians had finished.

But the prophets of old, of the exile, they kept telling us that it would be good, that you would reward us, that your messenger, your Messiah, would come. So where is he?

Well, I'm here, Lord. Malachi, your messenger today, and you keep telling me that your prophet is indeed going to return.

What would Elijah say to this people, Lord? This people just 40 years into the New Jerusalem? Just 40 years since the long walk back from Babylon?

He would say that our worship is half-hearted. That we offer sacrifice, but still do not accompany our sacrifices with justice and mercy. I can see why the people are like this, Lord; justice and mercy are hard, and costly. Sacrifice is relatively easy – I come along, the priest says the words, I give my money and home I go. But justice and mercy involve a change of heart. A reorientation, a repentance. That's hard work, and it makes a difference to me before it makes a difference to the others. People can't be bothered with all that work, and besides, you might ask me to do something I don't want to do . . . No, they say, sacrifice for sin is what the Lord has always required: neat, tidy, over and done with. Why change our ways now?

Elijah would say that we are a people with no standards. That we have come once again to believing that you live in the temple, not among us. We shut the temple up at night, slamming the doors shut tight, with you trapped in there. And what we do behind our closed doors is up to us. But that's not so, is it, Lord? We focus on you in the temple, but I know you're just as real here, at my desk, as you are in the temple.

And Elijah would also say that although he was here, he is not the Messiah. That he is a forerunner of the real thing, a bit like a warm-up artist; although I don't think you should quote me on that, Lord.

That you will be sending the one to prepare the way, and then the Messiah will come.

Elijah would say to us that we know what needs sorting out. We know where we go wrong; and that you, Lord, you still want justice and mercy in all our doings, in all our relationships, in all of our lives.

So be it. Come, Lord. Come and bring your justice and mercy to my life.

May the sun of righteousness rise indeed, with healing in his wings. And may that healing apply to all the hurting and sad people that live in this world, and in this place.

Reflection

Use the last paragraph as a prayer for today.

Prayer

Come, Lord.
Come and bring your justice and mercy to my life.
May the sun of righteousness rise indeed, with healing in his wings.
And may that healing apply to all the hurting and sad people who live in this world, and in this place.
Amen.

11

Joseph's tale

Matthew 1

I'd always known Mary, since she was born. Her family lived next door to me and Rachel, and I remember Mary being born herself: the joy she brought to Jacob and Anna after all those years of waiting. The faraway look in Mary's eyes as she dreamed her dreams of the past and the future, but rarely the present. Too heavenly minded to be any earthly use, was how Rachel's mother described Mary when I told her – but then she would, and I'm running ahead of myself.

Rachel was a good wife, and we had many happy years. You see the boys? Big, strapping boys she bore me. And the girls were tough and shrewd, a bit like their mother. That is, apart from Susanna, the last baby Rachel bore; for Susanna's birth was her mother's death. Susanna was small and delicate, sensitive; not physically, but she was different. It's as if she knew the cost of her life was that of her mother's . . .

After I lost Rachel, Mary was often in the house, sorting for me and the children, so it seemed inevitable that I should ask for her to be my wife. She loved the children, and I knew I loved her. Shy and quiet, she would come to life when telling her stories to my brood: More! more! Aaron would shout, and she'd laugh and sometimes tell another, sometimes not. For all her quiet, unassuming way, she always had the upper hand. You couldn't know Mary and not love her – there was no guile or badness about her.

Jacob was delighted when we were betrothed. Mary had been sad after Anna had died, and he was worried about caring for her – and he was showing his age. So we were duly betrothed; and then the trouble started.

I shall never forget her face, as she told me the story – an angel, she said. Special baby, she said. The Messiah.

I won't tell you what I said as I stormed out to my workshop to whittle some wood and decide how to get out of this one. Except – there was a visitor in the shed. A man, who spoke of things I didn't understand, with an authority I couldn't question. The baby was special. The baby was . . .

The baby was due in midwinter. We had to go to Bethlehem to be taxed in midwinter. For all her dreams, Mary could be very practical. She'd seen enough childbirth to know what was going to happen. We travelled with the swaddling bands and goodness knows what else, all in a little pack. The donkey bore her weight willingly – that donkey adored her, and the boy after he was born. But when we arrived come nightfall, and the pains were upon her, nowhere had any room, despite folk seeing what was happening. All drunk and busy. Go on, they said. Try next door.

Thank God for the innkeeper's wife. She saw and she understood. 'Quickly,' she said, 'round the back – we've a lean-to you can bed down in. She needs to get somewhere or that baby'll come in the street.'

She wasn't far wrong. The woman assisted Mary at the birth, and within two hours he was born – big, loud and very, very beautiful. But then, all babies are.

She went back to the inn, and came back with some food for us both. The donkey settled down to sleep, and so did we. But then the shepherds arrived.

Shepherds, in Bethlehem. They'd left their flocks on the hillside – said they'd been told to come to Bethlehem to worship a new baby. And there they were. How did they know? Angels, they said.

We stayed on for a couple of months. Mary took a while to recover from the birth, and it was cold for travel, so I did some repair work around the town, and we left when we felt better.

I sometimes wonder about that woman. The innkeeper's wife. I lie here now, at the end of my life, and hope that she was rewarded by the good Lord for the kindness she showed us that night.

Joshua, whom most people call Jesus now, he grew into a dreamer, like his mum. A teller of stories, but a loner. He never married – said it wasn't for him. He's a fine carpenter, mind you. I wonder what he'll do with his life. I know his brothers and sisters love him, as does Mary – for he was her only babe. Despite all our long years together, happy ones too, she never bore another babe. Without that innkeeper's wife, I wonder if he would have survived – or his mother. Small kindnesses can be large kindnesses – depends on your perspective.

Soon I shall sleep with my fathers, and Mary and Joshua, and the others, they'll go on. On into a future that I won't be part of . . . I shall watch from the other side, and see what life holds for my Mary and her Jesus.

Reflection

You might like to read the poem 'The Innkeeper's Wife' by Clive Sansom (*The Oxford Book of Christmas Poems*, Oxford University Press, 1988).

Pray for all the babies who will be born today, and in particular for babies born to parents who are homeless.

Pray too for families who will lose their babies today, through illness, starvation, or through violence.

12

In the stable

Luke 2.1–7

They say that life is like a tapestry – you can't make out the pattern when you're in the middle of it, but when you look back, then you can see the picture. That's been so for me – the little things that happen, that build up to make the big picture . . . it's been an amazing life, one that friends ask me about and they never seem to tire of the stories. Because, you see, I was there.

I worked for the master for many a year before he married again. His first wife died, and he and the children managed so well together – his eldest daughter, Sarah, she just took over and ran the household. He only thought about marriage again after the two of them – Sarah and Ruth – were both married and settled. I knew he'd liked Mary for years; he'd watched her grow up with Sarah, so I wasn't surprised when he made an offer.

And Mary was a lovely girl – helpful and kind, hard-working too, and would be a good wife. He had his head screwed on, did Master. But things went wrong at one point – lots of gossip and rumour about Mary, but Master, he stuck by her, and said he would marry her no matter what.

And so he did. A lovely, quiet wedding, for round here, what with Mary being in the family way and all . . . but she came and lived with us, and settled down really quickly. Master worked hard, what with more mouths to feed, but he was so skilled at his work, he had no trouble finding it.

Time went by. Mary, she grew rounder and rounder, and had to waddle around the place towards the end. I thought the bump suited, but others couldn't believe such a tiny thing could get through the birthing with a babe so large.

And then the real disaster struck. The Romans, the soldiers who strut around and generally annoy folks, they demanded we went to Bethlehem, to enrol, to pay them money for occupying the land. Well, I dunno why everyone just did as they said. Bertha, who I share with, she said that if the folks didn't do what the Romans said, they had their houses burnt down, so that's why they do as they're told. Master gets me to obey by giving me extra food – that's my sort of persuading . . .

Master was in such a state. You can't travel in your condition, he kept saying to Mary, but she just said, well, there's nothing else we can do – I'm sure it will be OK.

But I'm thinking, what about the baby? . . . and so were they, but they didn't say so.

Time came for the trip. Master, he got me out, fed me well, and said I'd have the hardest job of all. Then I realized: I was going to have to carry Mary – she couldn't walk.

Well, you folks seem to think that we can just carry everything you put on our backs, but we can't! We have our limits too! I'm thinking – if I have to carry her, and that lump, all the way, I'll die when I get there!

But what could I do? Mary looked me in the eye, stroked my nose. 'Come on, Raff, I'm sure we can do this together,' she said. Together, my hoof. Who's going to carry *me* when I drop?

She gently eased herself on to my back. My life, but she was heavy! Master took what he could, but it was going to be a long way.

We set off at dawn, and travelled for days. We slept at inns on the way, joining up with more folk, all going to be counted.

And I managed the journey. A strange thing happened – as I travelled, so Mary seemed to weigh less and less upon my back. Each morning she'd get up again, heavy and struggling, and by the end of the day, she would feel like a feather. Made no sense, but it felt as if she was being carried by something else as well as me and my poor old bones.

So we arrived at Bethlehem; a weary sort of town, full of its own importance, but nothing special, for all folks crack it up to be.

It was full. People everywhere, all looking for somewhere to stay. No spaces even for me, let alone people. Mary never lost heart, but Master, I could hear his voice changing as he tried to find somewhere, anywhere, for Mary to rest. They both knew the baby would come soon.

In the end, they found somewhere for me, and they joined me in my lodging. It was just a stable, just like at home, shared with other travelling folks' animals, quite warm, and I thought quite OK. I know Master would have liked somewhere a bit less crowded, but they couldn't argue.

So it was that the baby came, in the night, as they do. Mary dropped him as easy as Bertha foaled, and she lay him in the manger, to keep him warm. We looked on – nothing special about a birth for us, but for Mary, it was her first time, and that's always special.

The babe was a beauty. Big, dark eyes, that looked around like he was expecting to be there anyway. Later on, men came, with sheep, to see the babe. Nothing unusual about a babe, I thought, but they thought there was something special about this one.

And then the baby looked straight at me, and I felt his gaze, and – oh, I know it sounds strange – I felt his love. And then he looked up, and I saw . . . twinkling lights. Round the ceiling, the rough roofing. Twinkling and glistening, and a tinkling sound, soft and shy. Then they got bigger – more twinkles, more sound, and I suddenly saw them. Angels, they're called. Glowing people, floating on soft swan wings, big ones and small ones, young and old, laughing and singing they were. I looked again, and they called to me, and flew across the space. And how they laughed – for sheer joy. They laughed and they laughed and they laughed. And, even today, I catch a glimpse of them. Bertha says once you've seen an angel, you can see them all over the place. And I know, I do.

So there we were, quiet, peaceful, waiting for the dawn, to see what the next day would bring. Deep in my addled brain, I had a suspicion that maybe this was a special babe, and maybe we would be going to more places before we went home finally, maybe I'd see more of the world than I expected. But if Mary was as easy to carry as she'd been on that last trip, why then, that would be just fine by me . . . and if the angels came too, then I'd be a fool not to go along with them.

Reflection

Think about all the hard tasks to be done today.

In your mind, lay these tasks into the palm of God, and leave them there.

Now spend a few moments relishing the lightness of your load, and celebrating God's love for you.

13

Epiphany

Matthew 2.1–12

I've worked at the palace all my life. I started as a camel hand, in the stables, but because I was quite well spoken, and learned quickly, I was transferred indoors, and found myself as footman to one of the rulers. They weren't kings, they were philosophers, but because they were so wise, they effectively ruled Persia. People would come and consult them, and the three of them would debate and discuss, throwing ideas around and sorting through thoughts until they arrived at what they felt was the best answer they could give. If I worked for any of the three, it was Melchior, the quietest, most reflective of them. Caspar was the most outgoing; he was often the man that people came and saw face to face. Balthazar was Caspar's younger brother, and he was less confident.

Melchior – well, he was Melchior; easy to work for, undemanding and some might say a bit of a dreamer. But it was often his voice that held the answer. The others valued Melchior highly.

It was Melchior who first saw the star. Oh, they were skilled astronomers, watching the heavens many nights of the month, observing and noting changes. Melchior spotted the star in the wintertime; it was new, he said, as it rose in the west, and twinkled on the horizon. It was a very white star – they're often yellow or red, but this one was white. Melchior was convinced it was a sign. But of what?

All three of them consulted their books, and debated long that night as to what this star could be auguring. They were still at it the next morning, as they bathed and then ate breakfast together. Melchior was pondering its significance, while Caspar was all for mounting up and setting off to follow the star – for, indeed, it did seem to be moving away, as if we should follow. Balthazar pointed out that if we were to go on a journey, we should at least pack some suitable clothing and food. And if the star was to show the birth of someone important, we should take gifts . . .

They discussed it all day, and then set up to look for the star again that night. And there it was, a bit further away tonight, but still shining in all its beauty. I could see what they meant – it seemed to be beckoning. Come on, follow me, I can take you to your hearts' desire . . .

So we did. It took three days to organize, because, of course, it wasn't just the three of them who were going. Servants, including yours truly; food, clothes, bedding . . . kitchen sinks were mentioned, but we didn't have enough camels, and besides, they don't like the plumbing.

So we set off, across the ancient land that we loved so well, heading, I thought, vaguely towards Egypt.

How long did it take? Truly, I couldn't tell you. We began with high spirits; but as time went by and we began to get truly saddle-sore, or footsore, and the camels were their normal helpful selves, our spirits began to fall. Summer came, and we were still travelling – I swear we went round in circles for one month – until we came to some provincial capital called Jerusalem. It was autumn by then.

Jerusalem – what a dump! People who lived there thought it was the ultimate in sophistication – but, well, what do you say! They need to try Persia, I thought. Babylon and Ur – now they're what I call cities. Turned out they had, many years ago, when the Babylonians ruled the world; even this place had sent exiles over to us. Didn't learn from their experience, is all I can say.

Anyway, we found the king. King! Egocentric, puffed-up idiot, I call him – but not to his face. Herod was one of life's nastier people, best left alone in his pride. Herod didn't know of any huge event in his country, but he called in their wise men, who consulted many ancient scripts. And so we were directed to Bethlehem.

It was a day away, that was all, and we crossed that little country with such joy. Maybe this was the end of our journey, maybe this was where the star would settle. For the star had indeed led us here, moving gracefully and slowly before us, as we travelled, like a friend.

The star stopped over Bethlehem. Little farming community, like we have at home. But clean and well tidied up, as if they knew someone important was coming.

The star was over a house. I know that sounds silly – how could we tell? But we could. It was over a house, and when we went in, we found a young woman with a baby – he was about a year old – and her husband. The baby was lovely – smiley and jolly, as they can be at that age. But when we saw him, we all knew. This wasn't any baby. This was a special baby, hidden in a run-of-the-mill house, with typical parents. Caspar looked at the others and smiled, then they all knelt down. They were completely overawed, and it takes something to do that to Melchior and Balthazar.

Mary, the woman, smiled, and welcomed us. A rough tongue, but charmingly spoken. One of us could interpret. We gave our gifts, which had seemed a strange choice as we left, but made perfect sense now.

Gold, for a king.

Frankincense, for a holy person, a priest or prophet.

Myrrh, to anoint him when he dies.

For he surely will. People don't tolerate goodness too well.

We went home by a more direct route, leaving out a return visit to Herod. I heard that he died quite soon after our visit. I also heard that people believed that he died as part of God's vengeance; for after we left, he killed all the babies in that little town. I wonder what happened to our baby, and his parents? Surely, he was too important to be wiped out by Herod's fit of jealousy?

I wonder who he became. I'm old now, not long for this world. I often look back at that journey and wonder – just who was that baby, and who did he become? Was he really as important as we thought?

I believe, perhaps, he was.

Reflection

As you go through the day today, ask God to show you how much he loves the people that you meet, see, queue up with, rub shoulders with.

Analyse how that makes you feel differently – towards the other people and towards yourself.

Ask God to help you to greet everyone in the way that you would have them greet you.

14

The slaughter of the innocents

Matthew 2.13–23

That's her grave, friend, the one over there. There's quite a row of them, you'll notice. We lost 13 from this village: 13 babies and toddlers, all cut down for no reason other than the whim of a ruler feeling insecure. She was one of the last.

It was one evening. The children were just going off to sleep, the fire was low and we were just tidying up after the day, before settling to sit and watch the sunset, when we heard them coming. Not a lot of soldiers, but enough. They simply went into each house, and searched for small children. If there was a baby or a small child, they killed them, there and then, in front of the parents. We soon realized what was happening – the wailing and screaming came before the soldiers once they'd started. Women and men were dying too, throwing themselves in front of their children. Luke didn't. He knew that we needed him, and that if he died, then he would have been condemning me and the two others to starvation. So we stood and let them do it.

Sophia wasn't even a noisy child. She was a happy, chubby little tot, who smiled all day every day, sitting on my hip, or being fussed around by her elder sister, Ruth. She was the only one from this family; Ruth and Philip were clearly outside the age they had been told to take. Other families lost two or three children.

We heard the soldiers as they travelled through the next village, and all night, the sound of wailing. The next day we buried them all, side by side, asking God to take pity on their souls, and on the souls of the man who ordered this murder.

The trouble is, friend, I haven't told you when this was, or where this was. It could have been so many places – yes, Bethlehem, but how many children have died since then? And Moses himself was fated to such an end, if his mother had not been a clever woman. So, think, friend, of the other times that this has happened; times without count. I could mention some times: Warsaw, Berlin, Amsterdam, Vietnam, Biafra, Rwanda, Darfur, Bosnia, Chechnya, Afghanistan, Iraq, Burma, Eritrea . . . you want more?

So the soldiers continue to come, and the children continue to die in the wars of men and women, that children have no part in.

God forgive us and save us.

Reflection

Pray for parents who have lost children today, be they babies, toddlers, children or adults.

Pray that they may be comforted by the Father, whose own Son died that we might live.

15

John the baptizer

Luke 3.1–6

I have seen a miracle. Today, in the wilderness, I heard prophecy fulfilled, God's word spoken, and events long foretold coming to pass. May the Lord be praised, I live in remarkable days.

It is now 15 years since Tiberius became Emperor, and Pilate rules in Judea. Pilate's brother, Philip, rules Ituraea and Trachonitis, and Herod rules Galilee. May it make them happy to have such power, may they use it wisely.

Many years ago there was a rumour of strange events: of a star, and men from the east seeking a king – a child. Herod certainly believed their story, for he killed all the babies in Bethlehem that year – my cousin lost a child in that dreadful massacre. There were rumours of angels and strange births – but then, there are rumours all the time in this country. If these stories are true, the babies in these stories would now be men; men able to undertake the role God has given them.

It's in the prophet Isaiah, you see, as well as Jeremiah. Words of hope, words of God returning to us. Words of his servant, words of his life and his hope.

The voice of one crying in the wilderness. Prepare the way of the Lord.

All flesh shall see the salvation of our God.

Hallelujah. Today this prophecy came true.

Today, I went out to the wilderness near the Jordan. I had heard – more rumours – I had heard of a man, John. He was out there, they said, he was out there speaking of the salvation of our God. Making way for the Lord.

I didn't believe it at first – as I say, rumours are our speciality here. But people went out, and came back, changed. Not slightly different, but . . . transformed. They said that John was preaching – harsh preaching too, about how our faith wasn't enough. How we needed to repent, to change our ways, to return to God. People were going out to John and being baptized by him in the river. Baptized as a sign of new life, of a new way of being. And it was changing them. They came back full of hope, full of expectation, expectation of the Lord's coming, soon.

So I went too. I walked, with the crowd, down to the Jordan. And there he was.

John's a big man. He's strong, and his face is passionate and animated. He knows. He knows about God, and he knows God. And he was standing, by the edge of the river, preaching to the crowd who were already there.

What did he say? I can't remember. I just remember knowing, to the depths of my being, that scripture was being fulfilled. John is the one who is the voice in the wilderness, the one for whom we wait. The voice foretelling the Messiah.

I was baptized too. I now wait, for the Messiah to come. May he come soon, and deliver Israel.

Reflection

When was the last time you went to a baptism? What change did you see in the life of the person being baptized? Or in their family if it was a small child?

Pray for all those who will be baptized soon, that the Spirit of God may enter the hearts and minds of all those who witness the sacrament being administered.

And give thanks for this great point of outreach within the Church today.

16

The baptism of Christ

Matthew 3.13–17

There are many events in my life that, when I look back, sound very strange. But for me, who was living them at the time, they were part of the same; a life that was full of seemingly odd events. Odd events that, when you put them together and see the pattern, make perfect sense. My mother had a saying about lives like mine; she used to say that life is like a beautiful tapestry. When you look at the whole it is a wonderful sight, but if you're weaving it, thread by thread, you're too close to see the overall picture. It can look messy and muddled, as if it will never grow and take a lovely shape. But then, at the end, you look back and wonder at the beauty you see before you. Well, so is my life. Messy, hard, sad at times, joyous at others. But now, when I look back, a picture is there that makes my head spin and my heart lift.

I grew up in a small village, much like all the other villages around. My father was a shepherd, and we lived a frugal but happy life together. When I grew up, I too followed the sheep and lived out in the fields. But this happened one day when I wasn't with the sheep.

I'd heard about the baptizer. John, the prophet, the seer, the madman according to some, and so I thought I'd go out, into the desert to the oasis where John was baptizing and preaching. My, how that man hated the hypocrites of the synagogues and temple! He rounded on them as if they were stealing his very soul! His tongue lashed them so I was amazed they ever returned. But they did – the same ones could be seen there day after day. Were they just there to check up on him, and ignoring what he had to say? Were they covering their own backs in case someone on high decided John had a point? I'll never know.

What I do know, though, is the story of the third time I went to hear him. And although I had been before, I never tired of hearing John. Like his cousin, he had a way with words that held you as you listened – a rhythm in his speech that was music to my heart and my soul. He was telling folk to repent; and that there was one who was to come before whom he would be nothing.

Well, we all knew about the one who was to come – the Messiah, the chosen one of God. We'd heard about him with our mother's milk, and we were hoping he would free us from the Roman curse that we lived with day by day.

Some people were indeed going down into the water to receive the baptism. It was a still, quiet day, and the sound of the river and the water as they went under was clear through the air. And then someone else came down, who John clearly knew.

'You?' he asked. 'Why should I baptize you? You should be baptizing me, cousin . . .'

But the man replied clearly, so we could all hear: 'Let it be so. It must be done.'

John clearly wasn't happy with this, but he continued. He took the man in his arms, and pushed him under. They came up together, water running down the stranger's face and hair. As they surfaced, so they looked at each other, full in the face. And the expressions have stayed with me ever since: John was radiant, but sad, with a hint of finality there. And the other? Well, he was radiant too, but with an expression as if he was looking through John to the future, as if he could see years ahead; a hint of pain and sadness, while at the same time almost a pride.

They stood there, just for a moment, and then it thundered.

Yes, I did say it was a calm, still day. No one saw the thundercloud forming, but there it was. No lightning, just the rolling boom of the sound.

Both John and the other man, they looked up to see the noise, and some said it wasn't thunder, but a voice. What the voice said is not my part to tell – as I said, I heard the roll of thunder. But others said it was the voice of the Almighty himself, expressing pleasure at the work of John that day.

What I do know is that the stranger paused for just a moment in the water, then he turned and walked off, into the desert. Not the way he had come, from Nazareth and beyond, but into the desert that leads nowhere, other than to the barren heartland. I didn't see him again for a while, and then it took me a while to recognize him – but now I'm heading off into another tale.

You keep this one in your head, listener. Who was that man, John's cousin? Why did it thunder over this baptism? Was it just coincidence? I thought so at the time. Now, I guess it may have been the voice of God.

People change with time. The stranger, he changed, and so did I. And those changes were tied up together.

Be wary of going to watch a prophet. It can change your life.

Reflection

Think back to a time when God moved deeply in your life.

Reflect on the changes that movement brought and how that has affected your life, and give thanks for your spiritual journey.

17

The death of John the baptist

Mark 6.14–29

You ask me what it's like to work here?

I tell you, no self-respecting Jew should ever work in this den of thieves and sinners. Herod – King Herod as he likes to call himself, but he's no king, not like his father, Herod the Great. He's a tetrarch – rules Galilee and Perea, fair enough – but 'rules' is an interesting word. The man's got no respect for our ways at all: he built his city, Tiberias, on an ancient burial site, so no Jew can go there without becoming ritually unclean.

That's one way to get rid of us. He hates the Jews. He likens his court to the imperial court in Rome – but surely it's got to be better there!

So, no Jews in Tiberias, and if I go there I have to go through ritual cleansing before I can visit my family.

Then there's the wife, Herodias. No spring chicken is our Herodias, and my, can she hold a grudge. Got the memory of one of those elephant things that I once heard talk about. She was married to Herod's half-brother, Herod Philip, but she got fed up with him, and proceeded to marry our Herod, Antipas. Sadly, his half-brother is still alive, so that's no marriage in the eyes of Jewish law.

And John the Baptizer heard about the marriage. Herod was always going off to hear John speak, he couldn't keep away. So it was inevitable that John should hear about Mrs Philip becoming Mrs Antipas in quite a short period of time, and he said, straight out, that it was sinful.

Herod, he would have talked about it with John, tried to explain, for there's always a reason for what he does. Frequently it's that he just wants something, so he goes and gets it, but there is always a justification in Herod's head. But Herodias, she heard about it, too.

She's got thin lips, has Herodias, and from time to time they get thinner. Well, when she heard about John saying that her marriage was sinful, her lips vanished. Her eyes went cold and steely, and I thought, that's it; trouble's coming.

A few weeks later, I heard that Herod had arrested John, and put him in the castle at Machearus, our summer residence near the Dead Sea. I also heard that John had been arrested to keep him safe from Herodias, who has been known to slip a soldier a denarius or two to facilitate the disappearance of an enemy.

So we decamped to Machearus too, as the heat rose.

The hangers-on hung on and came too. Herod loves company – keeps his conscience quiet and him distracted. It was a lovely summer. The court went hunting and did all the other things they like to do to ape the court in Rome. We all ate, drank and were merry.

Herod's birthday falls in the summer. I don't know how old he was – about 45 I think. Herodias had just turned 40, despite claiming to be less than 35. Herod was looking his age. The business with John had unsettled him, and he was perturbed by John's speech. If he hadn't had that wife, he would have spent hours in John's dungeon, just listening. Poor Herod. Like many men of these days, it's the wife who runs the court. Just like her mother-in-law before her.

So, it was the birthday. Herod had the usual feast, with the hangers-on and the so-called 'top men' of Galilee. Top men – pompous idiots. If they weren't so dangerous, us servants would laugh at their overblown egos. But no, we keep our heads down, and so keep our heads attached to our bodies. Unlike other people.

They'd all had plenty to drink, and Herodias was plying Herod with wine – she was plotting, was Herodias, and we could see that. She whispered in Herod's ear at one point and he burst out with a shout of approval. A few moments later Salome, Herodias' daughter from her previous marriage, came in and danced.

Not exactly plain, young Salome. Just coming up to marriageable age – her cousin James was after her – she came in and danced.

I don't know what she thought she was doing. Usually we employ servants to dance like that, and then to give the men pleasure. Salome didn't take part in the pleasure bit, but she did do the dancing. And her stepfather loved it – mind you, he was so drunk I'm amazed he could focus!

At the end, as she collected her veils, her stepfather greeted her loudly and asked what she would have as a reward.

Now Salome isn't like her mother. She hadn't expected a reward – she was actually quite fond of the old fool, and may well have danced just because she thought Herod would be pleased. As he was, but when a ruler offers you a reward – well, Salome went for some help from Mother at this point. And so the plotting came out. John the Baptist's head, on a platter. After all, it's a feast.

Herod was stunned. Absolutely sober in an instant, as he saw how his wife had run rings round him yet again.

So it was that John died. He died with dignity, in a cellar under a castle. I let his disciples know, and we arranged for his body – and his head – to be buried, down by the river Jordan where he had spent so much of his time.

John's cousin, Jesus, he picked up the mantle John left behind, and Herod continued to live in fear of the prophets who seemed to haunt him.

All that power Herod had, but nothing could ease his guilty conscience. The truth, as John spoke it, had pierced his soul, and he was never at peace. So John never really died – the power of his words, they lived on. God's spirit continued to call Herod to repentance, but Herod never had the strength to do it.

Reflection

Is there anything in your life that comes back to haunt you?

Could you make amends for that action, perhaps by meeting with a person that you hurt? Writing a letter, making contact?

Pray about that situation now, and ask God's spirit to give you the wisdom to make amends.

18

The healing of Bartimaeus

Mark 10.46–52

They say that the walls of Jericho have been the same since they were rebuilt after Joshua knocked them down all those years ago. I'm convinced that they were destroyed in the great siege before the exile to Babylon, but then, who am I to judge?

I wasn't born blind. I went blind when I was six – an accident with a stick that got poked into my face by another child. So I missed being able to see; I knew what being able to see means. Sighted people can work and I couldn't, because I couldn't see.

So I was the only one in my family – my parents, brothers and sisters, they all saw. It's a strange thing, being blind – you forget what people mean when they talk about colour, light, beauty. I knew whose voices I liked, and I had friends who allowed me to touch their faces, so I knew in my own way how they differed from other people. But many words come to have no meaning for me at all.

And, as folk say, I do have an acute sense of hearing. Not so much sound as intonation. I can spot a liar at 100 yards! Something in the way the voice modulates, something that rings bells in my head, tell me that a person isn't being straight with me.

But I missed school as a child – not that my brother learned much there – and obviously, I can't read. I can't work, because I can't see what I'm supposed to do. I can't farm as I need to stick to a small area that I know in my head. If a trader moves their stall, I'd walk into it as I travelled to my spot each day.

Yes, I had a spot. I sat there each day. My brother Thomas took me at dawn, before he went off to the fields, and he took me back to his house as the sun set. I know I said I didn't work, but I suppose in a way, I did: I begged.

I sat at my spot every day. It was a good one, as it was shady in the heat of the day, and people tend to walk on the shady side of the street. I was just outside the city, so lots of travellers went by – they have to enter the city through the gate up the road if they're coming in from the south. I'm told I looked appropriately pathetic, and I was certainly a bit smelly. Thomas told me I had to look poor. That's not hard, as I am.

There had been a lot of people around that day – perhaps you know what went on?

What's that – the teacher's coming this way, today? The teacher that heals? The teacher that folk say may be the Messiah – even though they whisper that for fear of the Jews?

When's he coming – do you know? Soon? Soon! How soon? Where? Will he pass this way? In front of me? You say so – how will I know when it's him? You think I'll just know? Will you tell me if I can't tell?

You say the crowd are approaching now? Wait – yes, I can hear them! How long now? How long? I can't hear you for the noise!

Jesus, Son of David, have mercy on me!

Son of David, have mercy on me!

What's that – he wants me? He wants to speak to me? But – he can't! He's got far more important people to talk to than me!

'Where is he? Take my hand, please, lead me to him, will you?'

'What do you want me to do for you?'

'My teacher, let me see again.'

Soft hands on my eyes. Hands taking my face, like a butterfly's wings over my eyes . . . light burst in on my mind. I squinted and closed my eyes – the light was too bright, it hurt . . .

Then I opened my eyes, to look into another's. Soft eyes, full of love and laughter.

I could see. I could see. I could see. Thank you.

He smiled, turned, and began to walk off, along the way he was going.

I sat stunned for a moment, then I picked up my change, my wrap, and leapt off after him. I'm coming too. I too shall walk in the way.

Reflection

For sighted people: How much do you take your senses for granted? Look out, and enjoy the view, no matter what it is, for you can see it. Thank God for the beauty of the world around you, and pray for those who are losing their sight.

For those with no sight: Pray for people who can see, that they might recognize the difference that you bring to the world. Thank God for the beauty of the world, and for all that you enjoy of it.

19

Zacchaeus

Luke 19

I've been with Zacchaeus all my life – my mother was his kitchen slave, and I'm, well, I guess I'm like his personal manservant. I take care of him – make sure his clothes are clean and smell nice, wash him day and night, and perhaps almost the most important service, I guess I'm what you would call a bodyguard. I take care of him while he's out, taste his food and drink, and keep the bad 'uns off him. Oh yes, he is attacked from time to time, when folks think they've been short-changed. But then I always say – what do you expect? He is a tax inspector, after all, and the Romans don't pay tax inspectors – they set their own fees!

His scale of charges has increased down through the years too. He thinks I can't count, but you can't do this job for as long as I have without something rubbing off; I can count as well as he can now! And many years ago, when he lived in a smaller house and had fewer slaves to look after him and the property, then he charged less. You might say it's greed, but I think he calls it 'lifestyle requirements'. Put it this way – if you've got to pay him your tax, make sure you bring plenty!

We live in the best part of town now, as you'd expect. No hoi polloi round here. Helps with the security, too, to live in an area where the Romans patrol from time to time. Jericho's an old city, though, with a long memory – there are times when I wish he'd rein in his appetite for the good life a little, and show a bit of understanding towards those who've come to him desperate. But it won't be me that suffers when someone decides Zacchaeus has extracted his last denarius from them – it'll be a clean pair of heels and I'm away. I've also learned how to save.

Today seems to be a special day for Zacchaeus; he's in quite a dither, not like himself at all. He wanted his best clothes, and we had a full wash and massage before we got dressed. He mentioned something about a new rabbi coming, and he wanted to go and hear him. Well, we don't usually bother so much with rabbis – we go to synagogue, as you do, but go to hear a rabbi? This man must be good! So we ate plenty of breakfast and set off.

He must have been good – the place was heaving, and it was hours before he was due to arrive. There were crowds lining the streets – better than the Romans got last time they marched through, even with their music and horses!

And the trouble is, Zacchaeus is so small – just about shoulder height to me. So he's strutting up and down – 'Let me stand at the front, my good man!' – just to be elbowed in the ribs (I was there, jumping to his side) and told to 'get out of it'.

Then I see the tree – a huge sycamore that stands in the market square. The old dears have packed the ground under it but there's always room upstairs, as it were . . .

But Zacchaeus turns to me and says: 'Are you joking? How on earth do I get up there?' Pointing at the best branch . . .

'Easy,' I say, and pick him up and put him there.

And with that, he smiles, rearranges his clothes and sits, breaking out the picnic we'd brought in case of a wait.

After what seems hours, I hear the buzz – he's coming, he's coming. I see dust in the distance, and people moving forward.

The procession begins with some tatty fishermen types coming through. Then, then, here he is – tall, graceful in a country way. He's stopping and talking to people. Calm, and self-assured. A lame man is thrust out in front of him – and he heals him! This man just gets up and walks! The next thing you know, blind Bartimaeus is there in front of him – and the rabbi heals him; he's been begging there for as long as I can remember! And Bartimaeus is laughing and crying, both at once, going off his head with joy at being able to see once more.

And then, then he's standing under the tree. Looking up. Looking up at Zacchaeus. That's not something people do very often.

'Good afternoon, Zacchaeus,' I hear. 'Come on down – I'd like to eat with you tonight.'

People mutter. I get him down, and off we go, through the crowded streets, home; to eat and drink and for the rabbi to spend time with my master. Imagine that – why would he want to wreck his reputation in this way?

I don't hear the conversation – I withdraw with his disciples and we eat and drink. They tell me stories, bragging – surely he can't have done the things that they say he has?

But what happens to us is this. The next day, Zacchaeus begins to repay everyone that he has swindled – and that takes a long time. I don't know who that rabbi was, but he changed this house for the better, and Zacchaeus is a different man. Glad to be alive, glad to share, to give. And I am glad too. For we now have back the man that I remember from many years ago: restored, maybe I could even use the word redeemed?

Reflection

How important is your 'lifestyle'?

Reflect on how much of your money is spent on the latest fashion, shoes, gadgets.

Are these things really necessary in your life? Pray about them now, and listen to God's replies.

20

Peter's confession

Mark 8.27–38

It's funny, isn't it, where life takes you?

I grew up in a small fishing village on the Sea of Galilee. I was a good Jewish boy and attended school and learned my letters, as well as the Torah, and I knew the prophecies about the Messiah. We knew the Messiah would come as King; that he would drive out the Roman oppressors; that he would rule for ever as David had ruled all those years ago. That swords would be beaten into ploughshares. The lion would lie down with the lamb. Well, the last two were a bit poetic, in my opinion, but driving out the Romans, that surely was the Messiah that we needed, and that was what we looked for and waited for.

Now, looking back, I remember that when Andrew came running back, that day when it all began, he had shouted, 'We have found the Messiah!' I didn't remember that for a long time. Quiet, thoughtful Andrew had seen it long before I did. He'd always doubted what the Messiah would do regarding the Romans, saying that the Messiah wasn't here to gain an earthly kingdom for God, quoting the prophets and telling me to think again. But it was no use, because it's taken me a long time to learn how to think before I speak, and that day was a fine example of that.

My mum, and my mother-in-law, sometimes called me Simon foot-in-mouth, because that's what I do. Every time I open my mouth, some fool speaks, and Jesus knew that well, and he loved me despite some of the outrageous things I said. They never seemed outrageous as I said them – but he used to put me right; sometimes I felt proper told off too.

That day we'd walked to Caesarea Philippi. Herod Philip knew what he was doing when he built his capital there. Mount

Hebron, river source, lovely climate, fertile soil. The place was full of stuff about worshipping Caesar, not to mention the fact that the town desecrated an old cemetery, so we Jews hated going there; but it was a beautiful place, in lovely countryside.

We used to talk as we walked from village to village. Crowds always surrounded Jesus when he stopped, so we'd mosey along, chatting as we went.

He was asking about what the crowd were saying about him. There were always two sides to the crowds: the ones who were with us, and the ones who were waiting for Jesus to make a mistake, so they could prove him wrong.

'Who do people say I am?' he asked us.

Well, we'd heard people muttering – John the Baptist, the prophet Elijah, we replied. The usual suspects, all people from the past, who'd done what God had asked, usually at the cost of their lives.

He knew that, though. Jesus had heard the comments, the speculation. He didn't really want to know what the people thought about him. He wanted to know what *we* thought about him.

'But who do you say that I am?' he said, turning on his heel to face us.

I replied, as usual, without thinking about it. 'You're the Messiah, the chosen one of God,' I said.

His face changed as he heard the words. He then began to tell us not to tell anyone else.

Well, we didn't understand – nobody did at that point. If Jesus was the Messiah, then the whole world should hear about it, we told him. And he knew he was. It was as if he was just testing – to see if we'd got there yet in our thinking.

But then the trouble began. He started to tell us the truth. That he was going to suffer, and be rejected, and killed. He also said that he would rise after three days – but by that point I'd lost the plot completely. How could the Messiah be killed? He'd come to kill the Romans, not be killed himself. I lost my temper, something that I did on a regular basis, and began to tell Jesus that he'd got it all wrong – others might die following him, but he, he was going to be on David's throne in Jerusalem, that he was going to rule, that he . . .

Jesus was furious with me. No, he said, Peter, you've got it wrong, so wrong. Go away and calm down. We'll talk about this later.

So I went away, and tried to calm down.

Now, I see it all. The Messiah was not going to win us by big grandiose acts of war. Not by ruling in Jerusalem. Jesus came to rule in our hearts, to show us a better way. To love us into the kingdom.

It's so easy to understand now, but still hard to do. That the Messiah should suffer and die. That humans would kill the man who was God. That we should run away and forsake Jesus at his time of need.

But, as he said, he was the Messiah – but he called himself the 'Son of Man' after that. God became a man, to show us how to be, to show us how God is, to show us what the Messiah really was.

Reflection

Think back on a situation where you opened your mouth and said just the wrong thing.

How did you feel? Did you learn from that situation?

Reflect on that time with God – what is God saying through your embarrassment?

Have you overcome this tendency? Have you seen God work through your seemingly gauche comments?

What does this show you about how God works?

21

The Good Samaritan (1)

Luke 10.30–37

There's been a track here for as long as we can remember. Jericho was there first, of course – Jericho has always been there. It was here that the people learned how to farm wheat, and became settled. It was here that we heard the trumpets, then the earthquake, before the walls came tumbling down, as the song goes. It was here that Jesus healed a blind man – Bartimaeus, I think they called him, and he went off and followed Jesus, right to the end and beyond the end.

Jericho, one of the oldest towns in the world. We've seen so many invaders: the Jews, of course, on their way back from Egypt, as well as the Egyptians, the Greeks, the Assyrians, the Babylonians, and then the Romans. It was the Romans who put us here; before the Romans this was just a dirt track. Well used, pitted and holed. But a dirt track nevertheless. The Romans, they came and broke up the rocks, laid us stones in this beautiful pattern, so we meet, with a camber, making the road so good, and passable for chariots.

Of course, there have always been thieves along this road. What with the rocks to either side at this point, the thieves found it just what they needed. They hide behind them, they live among them, and they even live in the caves. And because it's rocks, there are no footprints. No tracks. Quick getaway, and on to the next spot.

We wondered at one time if the Romans would garrison some troops here, there were so many robberies, but it seems they decided not to. Not that the robbers are murderers, they rarely kill anyone, but I guess the Romans thought they'd lose men, and they can't afford to do that here. I don't know if all the countries they control are as unruly as this lot, but they certainly need all the soldiers they can find.

There was one robbery that I remember. Don't know why – they're all pretty much of a muchness. Man walks along the road, gets to this point, and wham! Over the rocks they came, bang, he's knocked unconscious, quick frisk of money and personal stuff, and away they went. Same lot as are here most days. They left the man, as they always do, out cold, but alive.

Several hours passed before anyone else came along. He was one of those posh folk, a priest I think they call them. Some rock told me that they were supposed to set an example, but this one didn't. He took one look, put his nose in the air and crossed the road. Good thing there weren't any robbers that side, I say – but then again, maybe not.

Along came another posh bloke, slightly different kit, from the other direction. He did the same thing – quick look, then over the road to the other side and a quickening of pace to take him on his way.

After that it was quiet for a while, then we heard the clip-clop of a donkey's hooves. It was a man who often travels this way, armed with a big club, which seems to put the robbers off. He never looks very well off, and the donkey could do with some hay, but he stopped. He looked at the man, and rushed over. He took some stuff out of his pack and put it on the man where they'd hit him. When the man began to wake up, he gave him some water, and put him up on the donkey. Then they went off, towards Jericho. Stones up the way said he took him to the inn just down the valley, and left him there to mend.

He's done that before, of course. He's the kindest man I've seen in these parts. Don't know any more about him, but I guess that's all you need to know – he knew how to help a man in need. That's the sort of person we like to have around. Shame there's not a few more.

Reflection

We often judge people by what they look like, their accent or their clothes. God looks at the heart. Pray today that God will help you to look past the exterior, to value the person within.

22

The Good Samaritan (2)

Luke 10.30–37

I was born and grew up, for a while, in Jerusalem. I was a good Jewish boy – did my daily work, went to the temple and the synagogue. I was even considered to be trained for the priesthood at one time.

But my life fell apart when I was eight. That was the day the soldiers came. Dad was working out the back. He was a carpenter, and had a shop behind the house, where people came and ordered furniture, had bits repaired and looked to see what he was making. 'Cos Dad was a good carpenter. He could tell you what tree a piece of wood had come from, and could look at a living tree and tell you what the wood would be like from that tree. He could coax wood to bend and be shaped, to shine and glow with his love. He made beautiful bowls; bowls for the table mainly, but just occasionally it would be a serving bowl size dish for the temple. Used in the sacrifices, those bowls were, and he would go to a sacrifice just for the pleasure of seeing his work being used. Everyone knew him, and he was respected as a good man, a man of his word.

So when the soldiers came, I assumed they wanted him to do some work for them. But they didn't. Someone had told them that Dad was part of an Iscariot plot – just imagine – and they came in and just took him away. They took him to the praetorium, where they beat him up, breaking his fingers just because they felt like it, and then left him out in the open. Nobody could help him on pain of similar treatment. So he lay out in the sun for 24 hours. Then he died.

What could we do? Mum went to live with her parents, with us tagging along. They took one look at all of us and decided that we needed to be apprenticed, so we were.

Amos, my older brother, he was apprenticed to another carpenter – he already knew the trade. Miriam went to a baker. I went to a blacksmith.

But I'm terrified of horses, and they were so big, the Roman horses. Every day there would be more of them. Beating the iron into a shoe. Burning myself over the brazier. Pumping the heat up with the bellows. Stoking, carrying, always round those huge horses . . . So, I ran away. I'd stuck it for three months, then one day a horse kicked me and broke my arm. My boss said it was my fault for being round the back of the horse, but it broke my arm. He strapped it up, but that was it. I'd had enough, and I ran.

I ran down the Jericho road. Not a place to go on your own at night. The gang found me when I ran out of running and went to sleep under an overhanging rock. So I learned a new trade; how to rob.

They fed me and cared for me while my arm mended. Then they taught me how to pick a pocket, how to trip up a walker and jump them. How to punch and hurt. How to knock someone out without killing them.

The first time, that's the worst. He was walking down the road, towards evening. We saw him coming from behind our usual rock, and waited. I jumped just after he'd passed, landing on his back, and down he went. Out like a light – must have done it just so. The others, they jumped in and took all his money, and we headed off.

It was a good jump; he was rich and I was rewarded with the best piece of lamb that night.

I don't know what happened to him – next day, he'd gone. Someone must've taken pity on him, 'cos it certainly wasn't the vultures that took him – they always leave some marks. No, some kind person must've come across him and taken him off. That's what I call a Godly act.

Reflection

Pray today for children caught up in criminal behaviour, and especially those working for adult gangs. Pray too for their families, and the victims of their crimes.

Remember children in custody, and those in care due to criminal activity, that God's spirit might enter their hearts and restore feelings of worth and value.

23

A leper reflects upon Naaman

2 Kings 5.1–14; Mark 1.40–45

Naaman had leprosy, but it can't have been as bad as mine. Perhaps it was only in the early stages when we read of him in the scriptures; he was living at home. Still working as a general – marching off into battle and winning; slaves as well as the fighting. It takes a while before you realize that it isn't going to clear up; that the deadness at the end of your fingers begins to reach down, into your heart, as you can no longer feel the softness of your baby's cheek, the silk of your daughter's hair. As you cut yourself shaving because you can't feel the pressure on your chin. It takes a while before the priests come and throw you out; out of your house, your home. Out of your village, away from all that you know. They give you strips of old clothes to wrap round your hands as they curl up into claws. They leave food at the city gates, to stop us from entering when the hunger becomes too much. Naaman's leprosy can't have been as bad as that.

Naaman was told by his wife to go to Israel and see the prophet there. He was sent with the king's blessing, to see Elisha, that great man of old. And Elisha didn't even come out of his house to greet the great general! Elisha just sent his servant! And what did Naaman hear that he had to do, to be rid of this dreadful curse? To dip himself in the Jordan seven times! Ha! No wonder he was cross! Go and have seven baths in our river! What! he said. The rivers in Syria are ten times better than this pathetic stream! And he turned around and headed back to Syria. But his servant – the servants make all the running in this story, first it's the slave girl from Naaman's wife's bedchamber, then Elisha's servant, then Naaman's servant, they're the ones who see what should be done each time – the servant just suggests, ever so gently, that it wouldn't hurt to try . . . just a quick dip in the Jordan before the long ride home, uncured, still with leprosy despite all our high hopes . . .

And Naaman does it. Seven quick dips in the muddy stream, and he comes out cured. So cured that he followed Elisha's God for the rest of his life. So cured that he went home and stayed home, with his family, and no one ever thought of him as a leper again.

And what about me? Five hundred years later, we still have leprosy. I still have leprosy. And I think I should go and see the new man of God, the new prophet that I heard about when I was sitting, still as a shadow, behind the town walls and listening to the gossip in the market place. He was called Jesus, a local man, and he's cured the lame, and the possessed. If he can heal them, perhaps, perhaps he could cure my leprosy. Let me go home to Elizabeth and the children once more; see their faces and feel their touch. Eat with them, share the Sabbath with them. Let me go home.

So, this morning, I got up before the dawn. I needed to be in town before everyone was about, or they won't let me in. I needed to hide, hide away and be still until Jesus comes this way.

Can you hear the noise? Is that him? Is that the prophet coming this way?

I see a crowd, with a tall man in the centre – that's Peter the fisherman, I hear he's with Jesus now. That must be Jesus there – he's coming this way.

Shall I? Can I? What will he say? How can I get near when I have leprosy? What can I do?

So, I stand up, and walk towards him. As people see me they scream with horror and back away. He doesn't, he just stands and looks at me, with a gentle expression on his face. Then he speaks:

'Friend, why have you come?'

'If you will, you can make me clean.' I just know he can.

And he smiles, gently. Love lights up his face, as he leans towards me, and touches my face.

'I will. Be clean.'

Lord, touch our lives, touch our hearts. Make us clean.

Reflection

Today it is often something other than an illness that drives people out of their communities; it may be shameful circumstances, or something from their past that has come back to haunt them. Christians with problems in their spiritual lives sometimes stop going to church because they think they will be judged by the others in the congregation.

Pray today for all outcasts, for whatever reason, that they might be healed and able to rejoin the community that they have left.

24

Bread and fish

Luke 9.10–17

Sit down, stranger, sit down, and welcome. Yes, I was expecting you – foreigners are rare in these parts, and foreigners seeking stories of the Master – well, you're the first one I've met! News travels fast. I know you were with Elizabeth last night, and James and Mary the night before. Tonight it's me – and tomorrow I'm sure you have another name to visit, another story to hear.

My, but it was long ago – I was but a lad, just shoulder height, but I can remember it as if it were yesterday. I'd gone to hear the teacher with my uncle – James, who you saw yesterday. The teacher didn't come to these parts often, and there was a huge gathering outside the town, on the edge of the lake, down by the boats, where they put in with their catch in the mornings. Mum had packed me up a huge picnic, enough to keep me going for hours, thinking that there wasn't anywhere up there that we could get food. The teacher, he stood up on the hill, and we sat down and watched and listened.

He healed first. Blind people were crying with joy. Deaf people were singing, lame people dancing. People who'd been crippled were able to move and dumb people were discovering the sound of their voices. Can you picture it? It was mad! But, eventually, everyone calmed down and we listened to him speak.

Did you ever hear him speak? No? – Your loss. A beautiful voice: a voice that caught your heart and carried it away. Even the birds stopped singing to listen when he spoke. And he spoke of the Almighty, of the Lord, in ways that I've never heard since. He knew; he just knew what to tell us – straight from heaven. And we sat and listened. Even that great crowd, even after all that excitement. Silence, beautiful, rich silence. The type you can almost reach out and touch. He spoke of love, of kindness, of humility. Prayer and listening. Living and being so people could grow.

I could have listened all day. In fact, I did! When he stopped, we realized that the sun was sinking, we were hungry, and it was nearly time to go home.

It was then that I overheard two of his disciples talking about food. Or the lack of it. They didn't have any food, not for them, not for the teacher; and best of all, he'd told them to find food for all the folks that were gathered – there must have been thousands! They were not happy, I can tell you!

'Where on earth can we find food round here?' one of them muttered.

'Some of his ideas – they're sheer madness,' said the other.

It was then that I stood up.

'Please,' I said, looking at the big one, 'I've got some food – would the Master like my supper? It's not much, but it's enough for me and him, I'm sure.'

'Very kind, I'm sure,' started the smaller one, but the big one, grabbed me: 'Well, at least there's something here,' he said.

So I was taken to him, the teacher. He was sitting down, clearly worn out after the day on the hillside. He looked up as we approached.

'Hello, Peter. Who's this, then?'

The big man looked a bit embarrassed and shuffled a bit. Well, this lad . . .'

'Surely, the lad has a name?' asked the teacher.

'Joshua,' I interjected. 'I've got some food for you. I'm sure my mum won't mind if you share my supper with me!'

'Well,' said the teacher, smiling and looking straight at me. 'Well, Joshua, that's very kind. What have you got in that basket of yours?'

'I've got five loaves that my mum made, and two fish, that's all, but I'm sure it's very good.'

'Oh yes,' he said, looking me in the eye, 'I'm sure it's very good indeed. Thank you, Joshua, thank you. Sit down, let's eat.'

So I sat down, and so did the other disciples. The Master, he blessed the bread and broke it.

Now this is the funny bit, so listen before you say I'm mad . . .

As he broke the bread and gave it out, there was more and more of it. At first, everyone was polite and took small portions, thinking we were on rations, but then they saw that it kept coming. And the same was true of the fish! Soon Peter, the big one, he was sent to find baskets from the crowd, and those baskets were filled right up with bread or fish, and handed round.

And the crowd did what we'd done – they were polite and took a little portion, but the baskets kept coming, and soon everyone was so full they could hardly move – all with my mum's barley loaves and two little tiddlers that I'd caught in the lake!

At the end, there were 12 baskets of food left for the seagulls. I gazed at them, and the Master stood beside me, with his hand on my shoulder.

'You see, Joshua. Our Father is generous when we trust him.'

I looked up; there was Uncle James, waiting to take me home. It was dark now – everyone was beginning to move off. I made to stay, but the Master, he scrunched down to look at me.

'Thank you, Joshua, thank you. What you did will never be forgotten.'

So we went home, Uncle James and me. And I've never forgotten, and I s'pose the people who were there remember the feast that we had, but I doubt if anyone will remember the boy with the five rolls and the two fish in the future.

So, stranger, was that the sort of tale you expected to hear? Is that the type of story you're gathering for your scroll?

We'll say good night, then, stranger. Your name was – Luke, you say?

Reflection

Many of us feel as if we have very little that God could use to help others, to reach them.

All this lad had was a picnic.

The trick is to offer what we have to God, and then see what God can do with it – for we all do have gifts, and they were given to us by God.

Jesus took something very small and turned it into a feast! What gift do you have to offer, that Jesus can transform for you today?

25

Peter's great confession

Exodus 1.8—2.10; Matthew 16.13–20

Every time I open my mouth, some fool speaks. That's what my mother-in-law says about me. I'm the one with my foot in my mouth . . . you get my drift. I'm always doing it. Sometimes it's helpful – someone, I think it was John, once said that I say what everyone else is just thinking. Fine, but I'm the one with the red face, aren't I? Sometimes it gets me into trouble. And just very occasionally, I think before I speak – and sometimes I regret that. But I'm rabbitting on, something else I do. Let me tell you about that day. The day when I opened my mouth, and a wise man spoke.

We were at Caesarea Philippi. Philistine country – way out to the west by the big sea, not our home Sea of Galilee. We'd been with the Samaritans who live that way. Jesus, he was doing his stuff – healing, speaking, getting people sorted generally. And we'd sort of got used to the amazing stuff he did. The first time I saw him heal a blind person I thought I'd never get over the shock, but now . . . And then, when he delivered a child from a demon; it's not just the child, it's the parents too. A girl or a boy, made normal, like the parents never could have dreamt they would be. Brings tears to me eyes, just thinking about it.

Teaching the like you've never heard. Every day.

It was the end of the day, and we were all tired. But no one got as tired as he did – so tired, he was only just there by the end of the day.

We ate supper – some fish that Philip had brought, with bread that I'd brought from home. We were just sitting, round the fire, like we did so often, when he said it:

'Who do people say the Son of Man is?'

We all looked at each other – we'd all heard the rumours. So we fed them back, trying to sound nonchalant: John the Baptist, Elijah, Jeremiah, or one of the other prophets . . .

We knew what else they said as well, but we weren't going to say it – not just yet.

There was a pause. He thought about it, slowly chewing his bread. We looked at each other, as we so often did when he asked things like this; did we know the answer to this one? Did he really want to hear what we were hearing every day now?

Then he looked at us. He had several ways of looking at us.

There was the peaceful, 'good job done' look.

There was the 'sort this one out' look.

There was the 'oh, my good grief' look.

There was the 'how long will you take to get to the truth' look.

And there was the 'please tell me what you really think, not what you think I want to hear' look.

This was the last one. He knew what people were saying. He wanted to know what we really thought.

'And who do you think I am?' he asked.

There was a moment. Who did we think he was? Who did I think he was, really?

And then I spoke – I hadn't framed the words or anything, I just said it. As I often do . . .

'You are the Messiah, the Son of the living God.'

I couldn't believe what I'd heard. Did I actually say that? Did I actually believe he was the Messiah?

There was a moment of pure tension as the others processed what I'd said.

And then I waited for the reply.

He looked down, and breathed out gently. Then he looked at me.

Which look would it be? The 'Oh, you fruitcake, got it wrong again'?

The 'Oh, Simon, think before you come out with such comments'?

The 'Get behind me, Satan'? – please, not that one again. But that was the one I expected.

He smiled. Beamed. Glowed.

Then he replied: 'Flesh and blood did not reveal this to you, but my Father in heaven.' And he didn't stop there . . .

'You are my rock, and on the rock I shall build my church.'

And he carried on – stuff about heaven and earth, powers and stuff. Stuff. That's all I thought it was. I'd hit the jackpot for once, and he was thrilled with me. The dunce's hat fell off, as I looked at him and felt my self-respect grow.

And he told us not to tell anyone else. That was the scary bit, because it meant that what I'd said was dangerous, not for public consumption.

But, at the end of the day, I realized that sometimes when I open my mouth, it's not a fool that speaks, but a wise man; wisdom that I now understand comes from God's precious spirit, and because I didn't think before I said it, I didn't have time to get scared and keep my mouth shut.

Oh, most of the time, it's still a fool that speaks, but now, with time, and all that happened, I've realized that if God gives you a word to say, even if it sounds odd, sometimes, you just have to say it. May not be what folks want to hear, but it may be what God wants to say. That's a scary thought.

Reflection

How often have you wished that God would speak through you?

How often does that happen and you don't realize it?

Reflect on the wisdom that you have, and ask God to help you to know when it's appropriate to share, and when it's better to keep silence.

26

The woman with the haemorrhage

Luke 8.43–48

It started when I was 13. I'd just been betrothed, having come of marriageable age, to John, whom I'd known most of my life. He's a fisherman, and I was quite happy to marry him – he's a good man, and I wouldn't want you to think that I blame him for leaving the betrothal. I think most men would.

I was betrothed on my birthday, and the courses started quite soon afterwards, and for three cycles, everything was fine. I hope I don't embarrass you with the details, but it's needed for you to hear my story and understand.

So I had three normal courses, just like I should. The betrothal had taken place and we were working towards the day of celebration when I would leave my family home and move to John's family home and become part of that place. But then I began to bleed, and it didn't feel the same. After three courses, I was used to the familiar draggy ache and feeling low and headachy, but this was different. I felt ill all over, and took myself off to bed. And I stayed there for three days, but nothing changed. So I tried to help with the work, but I felt so low I had to keep sitting down. And, of course, there's not a lot you can do outside the home for fear of touching someone else and making them unclean. So I did the cleaning and the cooking, but I felt so bad . . .

A week later it was still going on. My mother was beginning to wonder what was happening, but we're poor, and so we just assumed it would stop, as it usually did.

Another week later and it was getting bad. I was depressed and ill from losing blood, and fed up from not being able to see anyone. John wasn't allowed into the house as it was deemed inappropriate, and I didn't feel like seeing anyone anyway.

It continued. After three months, John was getting very impatient. Our celebration day had passed, and we were still betrothed and living apart. I was in bed much of the time as I felt so weak and anaemic.

After six months, John's family met with mine, and the betrothal was called off. We couldn't argue – how could he marry me? Until the bleeding stopped, I was unclean, and we all know women who bleed don't have babies.

After a year I was hardly able to leave my room. My father was old and looking frail, but I couldn't help support the family other than a little work every now and then. But I couldn't go out to plant seeds, shop or make the bread. I couldn't see friends or even walk in the countryside. I was too weak, and I was unclean. So I saw a doctor. Lot of use he was – told me to get some exercise, eat some meat and it would pass.

After another year, I saw another doctor. He repeated what the first had said. We couldn't afford for me to see any more doctors. My father died, and we became dependent on my brothers for bread and fish. My mother grew some vegetables in the field, and we had a goat for a while . . . we managed, just.

The years went by. John married my friend, Miriam, and they had three girls, I heard. But again, I couldn't go to admire the new babies, or even let John know that I bore no grudge. No grudge against him. But I did feel great anger at the Almighty from time to time. Here I was, bleeding to death. I'd been a good strong hard-working girl until this started, and now, now I was useless; a burden on my family and a drain on the resources.

And still the bleeding went on.

Twelve years passed. Mother and I, we got by, but life was only half lived. Until I heard about the preacher.

It was Miriam who whispered it to me through my window – a man who was said to have amazing powers to heal, even the blind or the lame. The deaf heard, and the possessed came into their own minds again.

'Go and see him,' she whispered. 'He could heal even your problem.'

Could he? Would he? How could I get anywhere near him when I was unclean? Why would he care about me, an ageing woman who'd lost the best years of her life through some horrid thing that had struck me down at the very point when life should have been getting better and better?

But, he was coming to our village, she said. Coming tomorrow.

So tomorrow came, and I woke early. I had spoken to my mother, but she thought it a waste of time.

'Why should this preacher care about you?' she said. 'You're a woman, and you're unclean. I don't think he'll want to know you at all.'

And I agreed with her. But, deep in my heart, I knew I had to try. To try at least to be rid of this dreadful thing that the Almighty had struck me down with.

I dressed carefully, covering my head and face with a shawl. I heard the crowd coming. I slipped out of the door, head down, being careful to pick my way along the backs of the people. I stood myself in the corner, where I could watch the road and the people . . . And here he came, tall and dusty. He was thin, with the usual beard, a crowd of supporters around him. People were stopping him to speak a word, to calm a worried soul, to help a questioning mind.

And he was past me, slowly walking down towards the synagogue.

I don't know why I did it, but I struggled out and walked up behind him – he'd stopped to speak to the leader of the synagogue, and people were fawning round him. But I could still see the hem of his clothes – perhaps, if I could just touch that hem . . .

I gasped as I felt the power surge through me, like a shock to my system, a punch in the gut. Immediately he wheeled round.

'Who touched me?' he shouted.

His followers tried to reason with him – for there was a big crowd by now, grabbing and jostling him.

'Someone touched me, I felt the power leave me,' he insisted.

I looked up. I straightened my poor body upright for the first time for 12 years and looked at him.

His eyes softened as he caught my look.

'It was me, sir,' I said. 'You have made me better. Thank you.'

'I have indeed,' he said. 'I have indeed. You faith has made you well. Go in peace.'

So I did. I went in peace. A peace the like of which I could hardly contain. Back to my mother. Back to life itself. Back to a new life; a life made whole by a simple touch.

Reflection

Many people live with debilitating illness for years without hope.

Have you something that is pulling you down, emotionally or physically?

How do you pray about it?

How do you cope if it doesn't go away? If it isn't healed?

Prayer

Lord, help me to live with the body that I have.
Help me to be generous towards those who are disabled and living in pain, be it physical or mental.
Make me open to be there for people in their need, to be your hands, your voice, your heart.
Help me to be there.
Amen.

27

The raising of Lazarus

Ezekiel 37.1–14; John 11.1–45

He never smiled again. No matter what we did, he always had that faraway look in his eyes; very like the look of a newly born babe, fresh from heaven. No matter what we asked, he never told. What was it like, Lazarus? What was it like to be dead?

You may have heard tales of my brother and my sister and me. They've been told among the people of the faith down through the years. Needless to say, these tales have grown and changed as they've been told, so maybe it's time that I told you what happened to me. If you can persuade Lazarus to tell you what happened to him, you can retire, I'm sure.

Mary and I, we'd often cooked and made house for the master. He stayed with us when he was in Jerusalem, and often as he came and went too. We were related, through his father Joseph, although I wonder about that too, now that things have turned out as they have. But he would come and stay. We'd cook, Mary and me, and we'd have a house full of people. We loved it. Yes, it did get a bit much sometimes – I dare say you've heard that story as well, but you know how it is; we were glad he was with us.

This tale begins when he was away, as he was most of the time. Lazarus had been working in the field, when he came home early. He was feeling hot and bothered, and he looked it too – you could have lit a fire off his cheeks that day, they were that hot. He went to bed, and we began to worry. If the master was here, he'd sort Lazarus just like that – we'd seen it so many times through the years. But the master wasn't here, and Lazarus, he just got worse.

That night we took it in turns to sit by him, and sponge him down, but the fever had such a hold. In the morning he was worse, so we sent word to the master, begging him to come back early and heal our brother.

He didn't come.

Perhaps he was too far away, and the message never reached him, but we thought we knew where he was. Surely, he would have come if he got the message – we knew that he cared about us deeply. Lazarus was like a brother to him.

But when he did come, it was too late.

Early one morning, three days after it began, I wakened in the early morning hush to see that Lazarus had left us. His body was still and grey. His struggle was over.

We buried him later that day, in the tomb that already held my mother and father. We wrapped him in our best linen, said the prayers, and closed the stone across the tomb.

He still didn't come. How could he not know? Did he not care?

Except, of course, he did come, but four days too late. I met him as he arrived in the village, and I told him, I told him, I said that if he had come, Lazarus would have been saved. Lazarus would still be with us, here with me, greeting him on the road. I ran up to him, and I collapsed, sobbing out my grief and anger at the one person who could have saved Lazarus.

And he smiled – that wistful, sad smile that I'd seen sometimes, as he seemed to go within and seek the answer there.

When I had calmed down, exhausted by grief and tears, Jesus sat down on the side of the road, and held my hand. Looking into my eyes, with tears in his own, he told me that Lazarus would rise again.

'Of course he will!' I cried. 'Of course he will, on the last day, at the resurrection . . .' And what good is that? was clearly discernible from the tone of my voice.

He said something so strange in reply; something that is fixed in my brain even today. And, with what came next, it makes all the sense today that it didn't then . . .

'I am the resurrection and the life. Those who believe in me, even though they die, will live, and everyone who believes in me shall never die. Do you believe this?'

I didn't even think about it. I just replied, sadly, 'Yes, Lord, I believe that you are the Messiah, the one who is coming into the world.'

I didn't think about it, it just came out. And as I said it, I realized what I was saying, and somehow I knew, I knew that I was right; that Jesus really *is* the Messiah . . .

But I was so embarrassed at what I'd said, that I ran to fetch Mary, and together we took him to the tomb. The gossips and busybodies, they followed, scenting a good story: after all, the Master was back – what would he do now he'd missed an opportunity to work some more of his healing magic? What he did do was a huge shock for all of us.

For he wept. He stood at the entrance to the tomb, and wept.

When he had recovered himself, he went to the tomb, and asked for the stone to be pushed away. We told him, it would be smelly after four days – did he know what he was doing?

He did. He knew exactly what he was doing. He stood at the opening and shouted down into the dirt and the mess.

'Lazarus, come out.'

And Lazarus did.

Reflection

You might like to read Gwyneth Lewis' poem 'VIII' from *Zero Gravity* (Bloodaxe Books, 1998).

Has God let you down recently? How did you deal with it? Did you tell God, as Martha did, how hurt and disappointed you were? Or did you feel that it was somehow wrong to be angry with God? Read Jeremiah 20.7–12 if you need some help.

28

The Pharisee's dilemma

Matthew 21.33–46

Dear Hezekiah,

I'm writing for some advice, well, help really. I'm in such a quandary I really can't see the way forward at all.

You know my family. You know how devout they are; synagogue every Sabbath, and how they sent all us boys to school to learn the Torah and scriptures. How proud they were when I enrolled at Pharisees' school, and then when I finished, with my robes, phylactery containing the law and my teaching role.

How proud they still are. Mamma said just the other day that it was her dream to have a son who became a Pharisee, and here I am.

I think that makes it worse, having them so proud of all that I stand for – because, you see, I'm wondering if I've got lost somewhere along the way.

I think about our past – right back to Abraham and Isaac and the Fathers. Of Moses and the people struggling through the desert, of the giving of the law, and then the great kingdoms of David and then Solomon.

I think about how it all went wrong – even though the priests were in the temple, leading the people. What did it feel like to them when the prophets came and denounced them and their work?

How did they cope when the temple was destroyed and the people taken into exile? The struggle to rebuild Jerusalem, Jerusalem the city of our Almighty God . . .

Could they recognize the hand of the Almighty in the prophets? In the Assyrian hordes? I don't know whether I would.

What is worrying me is the way that, every now and then, despite all our best efforts, we seem to lose the plot. We lose the voice of the Almighty, and he chooses to speak through someone else: someone who hurts us, offends our deepest beliefs and challenges us to our core. We call such a person a heretic, and we frequently get rid of them . . . but have you heard the latest one? I have. He chills me to the bone, because I think he may be indeed the voice of the Almighty; but somewhere I've lost the ability to hear what the Almighty might wish to say.

I heard him tell a story about a vineyard. Of how it was built, planted and set up. Of how the owner went away, leaving the vineyard in the hands of tenants. But the owner checked up on the tenants every now and then, sending slaves just to see how things were going. The tenants beat up the slaves, killed one, stoned another. He sent more slaves, and again they beat one up, killed one, stoned another. Then finally, so the story went, the owner sent his son, expecting respect. They killed the son. The story finished with the owner returning and having the tenants killed.

That's us he's talking about; we're the tenants. He looked straight at me as he said the words – and his look pierced my heart.

He finished by saying that the vineyard will be given to those who produce the fruits of the kingdom.

At another time, I heard the same man speak about the fruits of the kingdom; he listed them. Love, joy, peace, patience, kindness, generosity, faithfulness, gentleness and self-control.

Where are those things in my life? How many can I claim to be evident? Is this the true measure as to who is acceptable to the Almighty? If it is, then Hezekiah, I am lost.

I have decided to remove my trappings of being a Pharisee and follow this man, Jesus, in the way. Perhaps then I will be able, once more, to hear the voice of the Almighty.

In love.

Prayer

Lord God, help me to perceive your speaking to me, no matter how hard it may be to hear you using that voice.

Lord God, help me to put my prejudice to one side and to follow your call.
Lord God, help me to be faithful to you, no matter what.
Amen.

29

Palm Sunday

Matthew 21.1–11

You ask me how I know the story so well; well, I was there, you see. Oh aye, it was a long time ago now, but somehow, I've never forgotten that day. Or what came afterwards.

It was a quiet day. Same as normal, we had our munch of food, and then we started work. I was with my mother then, too young to work away from her; so the master used to tie me alongside, in the hope that I'd pick up the job. Or so the theory went. In those days, I wasn't the most co-operative of youngsters – a bit like you, I'm afraid, and I used to find lots of butterflies to gaze at, clouds to wonder about and grass to catch my eye and my tongue. Master would moan and tut at me, but he kept me despite it all. Perhaps he knew I'd be useful in the end.

Can't remember what we did early that day. Nothing exciting, and he'd tied us up by mid-morning with a nosebag, standing in the sun as the heat gradually increased. I love the morning sun on my ears; it always takes me back to that day.

As I said, it was a quiet day. Nearly Passover, Mum said, and that was a holiday, so we'd be in the field all day. It was the first day of the week, I remember, and as we were dozing quietly, we heard them approach us. Two men, talking and laughing.

'There they are,' one said: 'Those must be the ones he meant.'

They began to untether us, and our master came out to see what was going on.

'The Master needs them,' said one of the men.

'Ah,' said our master. 'That's fine, then.'

And they led us off, down the hill and back towards the village.

There was a group of men and women at the edge of the village, watching us coming.

'Not that one, surely,' a woman said. 'Jacob says that colt's useless – won't let anyone work him at all.'

A tall man, slightly apart from the rest, looked up. Then he walked round to us. He looked at us – not around us, at our legs and ears, like most men do, but at our eyes, right into us.

'Oh, I don't know,' he said, 'this is a lovely colt. I'm sure he'll be fine.'

He put his cloak on my back.

Normally, I would have begun to fuss right then; to buck and bray and get it off. It's a terrible feeling, that weight on your back at first. Feels like you're going to be killed, you know, and terror was going through me as he did it. I began to shake and tremble, for I knew, I just knew, that I wasn't going to get it off. Or him either. He wasn't like men usually are – he was different, and I could feel his concern and care for both of us.

So, when he gently sat on my back, I didn't flinch; well, not much anyway. I felt safe, and that's all I needed to let him stay.

My mother trotted along beside me as we climbed the hill to the city. The other men and women walked beside us, and I felt peace envelop us. The people were silent. Somehow, we knew something important, something significant, was going to happen, soon.

It did. As we reached the edge of the city, men and women began to gather. Children took branches from the trees and put them in the road for us to walk on. Coats and cloaks were there too – I felt like a Roman general's horse processing into the city that day. They began to shout out loud: Hosanna! Blessings on him who comes in the name of the Lord! Men and women ran alongside us. Excitement grew, and the noise grew with it.

Then, suddenly, it was silent again. We had entered the temple outer courtyard. The man got off my back, and patted me. He looked me in the eye, pulled my ear and said, 'Thank you. You can go home now. And look after your mother – she's a good animal.'

And so was I from then on.

We went home – one of the men took us, and tied us up where we'd been before. Master came out and looked at me.

'Well,' he said, 'was it a good outing, then?'

Reflection

You might like to read the poem 'What the Donkey Saw' by U. A. Fanthorpe (*The Oxford Book of Christmas Poems*, Oxford University Press, 1988).

Like the donkey at Christmas, this donkey knew what was going on, and understood far more than many of the people who witnessed the entry into Jerusalem.

How often do we assume that we know more than others? How often do we think that our way is the right way, the only way?

Ask God to let you see other people's motivations today, that you might come alongside them with a compassionate heart and mind.

Prayer

Lord, give me eyes to see,
Ears to hear
And a heart to follow you in the way.
Amen.

30

The woman and the oil

Mark 14.1–25

We were at Simon's house. Simon had been a leper until Jesus met him and cured him. Funny, that – we all met Jesus and were cured. Sometimes it was physical, like Peter's mother-in-law; sometimes it was mental, like Mary Magdalene; sometimes it was deep personal unhappiness, like me. Sometimes Jesus kept working at it, like Peter's pride and need to be noticed. But he loved us all, despite knowing, sometimes better than we did, what were our faults.

Simon was straightforward – he had leprosy, and Jesus touched his sores, and they went. It was, I have to say, awesome. To see Jesus touching an untouchable and loving him in such a clear, physical way. As his hands touched, the skin came up like new, like a baby's neck – you know, so that you just want to touch and feel the softness?

But there we were, eating and drinking together – it was fairly noisy that evening, the festival was well into its swing, and the worship at the temple that day had been lively and enthusiastic. We carried that mood with us as we ate, remembering odd moments from the day.

Then the woman came in. Now some say that this was Mary Magdalene, but it wasn't. Mary was with us when it happened – this was someone I didn't recognize, although she knew Jesus. She was carrying a beautiful alabaster pot, which she opened, breaking the seal to release the perfume inside, which she poured over Jesus head.

It's hard to describe the scene. I shall never smell that perfume again without seeing it in my mind. The smell filled the house. It was fantastic – pure nard; I'd hardly ever smelled it before, so clear and strong.

And the other thing was Jesus' hair. People don't talk about his hair because they get stuck on his eyes, but I loved his hair. It was long and thick, as you'd expect, but it was much more than dark brown, like mine is. In the light it sparkled and glowed, some deep red light that you didn't usually see. And if the sun fell the right way, his whole head would light up. His hair was long and glossy, although he wasn't at all vain about it. He would laugh and say, well, that's what it's like, and shrug his shoulders.

His hair had been back behind his shoulders, out of the way for eating, but as the perfume slid down into it, the weight came forward and it glowed even more than usual in the candlelight. It was a stunning sight – we all stopped talking and looked at him. We were all aware of his physical beauty, why Mary Magdalene was so in love with him, why people stopped to look at him in the street. There it was again – that powerful face, the steady eyes that held yours and looked into your soul, lit up by this mass of dark swinging, scented light.

It was as if a god was with us.

Then Judas started. He was always down on the women – probably because they so disliked him, and he set to with gusto. He berated this poor woman for wasting her money – wasting her money on Jesus! As if she could! But wasting her money on Jesus. 'It could have been given to the poor!' he shouted, right into her face.

But Jesus wasn't having that. With a gesture he shut Judas up, calmed him down. 'You always have the poor,' he said. 'She has anointed my body beforehand for its burial.'

What could we say? Anointed his body for burial?

We all started then – saying that Jesus wasn't going to die, what did he mean, what on earth . . .

And he sat and smiled at her – held her eyes, as he had done so many times before with others.

'Thank you,' he said. 'What you have done will always be remembered.'

But he didn't say by whom.

It was that evening, soon after, that Judas vanished the first time.

Reflection

We're not generally very good at worship in the sense that we see it in the above story. How could you worship more openly?

Spend some time sitting quietly, opening your heart to God. Offer your entire being; relax and let yourself go. You might find it useful to picture yourself in the palm of God's hand, just being in God's presence.

31

The washing of the disciples' feet

John 13.1–17, 31b–35

Water: strange stuff. Never enough of it in a household like this, and it's my job to make sure there is. So, most days, I go down to the well time after time. And some people appreciate that, and some don't. We had those children here the other day – waste, waste, waste. Worst thing is, I have to clear up the spilt water as well. So by the end of the day, I'm glad to splash some on my face, and go to bed. But I also like to wash my feet before bed, and many see that as a waste of water. But, after the Master was here, I see it as more a prayer than anything else – a way to remember him, and his friends.

It was Passover when he came, came to eat the meal with his friends. But it was dangerous for them by then; the priests had begun to wonder how they could be rid of him. He was upsetting the hierarchy left, right and centre, and they couldn't risk losing their Roman privileges. Being an official religion and all that, you have to watch your step with the guards, or you get relegated to behind closed doors – persecutions and deaths. No, they didn't want to risk losing their official status for Jesus and his friends.

Strange thing was, he didn't do it when they arrived; I'd washed everyone's feet as they arrived, as I always do. They'd sat down, and begun to eat. After a while, it went quiet. They were all wondering what would happen next. Jesus got up and beckoned me to him. Over I went, thinking he wanted me to run an errand or something. But no, he took off his outer clothes, took the towel that I'd used – it wasn't too clean by then – and tied it round his waist. He took the pitcher of water and my bowl from the stand, and went over to Simon, or Peter as he was known. Jesus knelt down in front of Peter, and began to pour water over his feet, and dry them. Not scrappily, as I must admit I did, but carefully, drying in between the toes like a mother does with her baby. Peter was horrified. He jumped up and shouted at Jesus.

'What are you doing? You don't wash my feet – the servant did that already!'

Jesus just looked. He often did that. Just looked. Then he slowly shook his head.

'Oh Peter, you don't understand.'

'No, I don't,' replied Peter. 'Do you want to wash my head and hands too?'

Jesus waited. Peter sat down, and Jesus returned to the task.

He washed all their feet. Carefully and with great attention to detail. He seemed to relish the contact. It was unbearably sad, and tense, as they watched and then waited for him to explain.

He put his clothes back on and sat down. To a man, they waited for him to tell them what on earth was going on.

He sighed.

Then he said something to himself, so quietly I don't think any of them heard it; but I did. I was standing in the shadows, where I always stood, waiting and watching.

'They're not ready, Father,' he said.

Then he turned and spoke; mainly to Peter, but so the others could hear.

'I am your Lord and teacher, you call me that. I wanted to show you that in the kingdom of God, there is no hierarchy. No one is better than anyone else. We are all equal before our heavenly Father. So, I washed your feet to show you that it is so. If I can wash your feet, then you can wash each other's. And anyone who needs his or her feet washing. In the kingdom, servants are with masters. Masters are with servants. All are equal.'

He sighed again. Then Peter sat down quietly. After a moment, Jesus gave Judas a piece of bread, and Judas took it and ate it.

He gave the others bread too, but I noticed that Judas left after eating his. He quietly went past me and out into the night. I remember noticing how dark it was outside.

They left soon afterwards. Others tell me that they went to Gethsemane, and we all know where Jesus was taken after that.

The others? No one knows where they went that night. Vanished, into the ground. I tidied up, and went to bed. It was the next day that I heard what had happened to Jesus. Did he know what was coming? I think he did. Whether he knew *all* that was going to happen – now that's a question I can't answer.

That night, Jesus went into the dark, and it stayed dark for him even after sunrise that Friday morning. It stayed dark for many of us too, those of us who watched, and waited, waiting for the sun to rise.

Reflection

How do you cope when people break boundaries with you in the way that Jesus did in this story? Do you adjust and smile, or do you respond in an aggressive way, trying to keep traditional boundaries in place?

Jesus wants his followers to be servants; how easy is that?

32

The garden of Gethsemane

Mark 14

If it were to happen again, would I do the same thing? I don't know. What would you have done? The question is, if we'd acted differently, if we hadn't run away – what would have happened then? Would the next few days have been the same?

What if? It's the great question. For me, though, I can only tell what we did, and hope he forgave us.

After the Passover meal, Jesus said that he needed to pray, so we went to the garden. He often went there – it was peaceful, away from the crowds, and he had his favourite spot there. We knew where he meant when he said, 'Let's go to the garden.' We'd been there before – and at night too. He had to recharge his batteries, after a day spent with all those people. And by then the people were beginning to wear him down – constantly demanding, without realizing how long the demands went on, day in, day out. He was tired, so tired.

So we went to the garden. He asked us to wait while he went on, but to stay awake. I dunno about Jesus being tired; we were all done in. We tried to stay awake, but we just couldn't. Peter was muttering in his sleep – Jesus had said that Peter would deny him, and Peter just couldn't handle it. Deny him – where could we be that Jesus would be challenged in that way? Why would any of us ever deny him? How naive we were.

Twice Jesus came back and found us asleep. I don't know if he was angry or frustrated or just beyond it. He woke us up, but we just went back to sleep again.

Then we heard the sound – the sound of soldiers, and a crowd; what were they doing here at this time of night? Peter jumped up – was this what Jesus had been alluding to?

Judas was there with them. He was looking jubilant, as if his time had finally come. Jesus had been on the ground, praying, but when Judas approached he stood up, and embraced him, as he would have any of us.

Judas embraced him, and his face changed. As he backed away, tears came into his eyes. Had Jesus said something to him? Had he realized his mistake? I don't know what happened, but Judas' world fell apart from that moment.

The soldiers came forward. They had ropes to bind Jesus, and at that point Peter screamed. 'No!'

He dashed forward, sword drawn, and attacked the high priest's slave. Fortunately he missed, and only cut off the poor lad's ear, but Jesus stopped Peter. Softly, he too said, 'No'. And then touched the bleeding wound. The ear was restored . . . how could this be?

But the soldiers didn't notice. Peter dropped his sword as if it was red-hot, and jumped back again, into the shadows with the rest of us.

And so we watched, safe in the gloom and the scrub.

They took Jesus away. And we turned and ran. John Mark even left his robe behind as he ran, and there he was, naked as the day he was born. But we were suddenly terrified – where would this lead? What would happen to Jesus now? And, more important, what would happen to us?

What would you have done?

Reflection

In your mind's eye, revisit the garden; what would you have done?

Spend some time praying about your reaction.

33

The Crucifixion

John 19.16b–42

I watched it all. I stood with Mary, his mother, and watched it all.

If you've never seen a crucifixion, it's hard to describe. Oh yes, you can say about the nails, about the humiliation, the flogging, carrying the cross up through the streets; but you can't describe how it feels when you're watching.

Jesus was tired before it all started. He was tired at the Passover meal, tired in the garden; and then, then he was up all night. It was only later that I heard the whole story from the women, but the things that happened! So strange – five days before, the crowd had adored him. Now they were baying for his blood. People. Who'd love them? Jesus, that's who.

After the arrest, he was tried by the chief priests, and then by Pilate. Pilate knew it was fixed, but what did he care? Anything for a quiet life. And if it hadn't been Pilate, it would be the next governor . . . Jesus had upset the chief priests, and they wanted him out of the way. Pilate knew it was either kill him or they would kill Pilate politically. All Pilate wanted was to get back to Rome – but not in disgrace. So he agreed. Washed his hands and signed the death warrant.

The soldiers took Jesus away and flogged him. They dressed him in an old royal gown, and taunted him. They shoved a crown made out of thorns down on to his head. Did they do it more because he let them? Because he just looked at them, as he looked at everyone, deep into your eyes and your soul?

Then he had to carry the cross up through the city. Not everyone was against him, though. Simon carried his cross – Simon of Cyrene. He was walking beside Jesus, quietly encouraging him, when Jesus fell, and he hardly had to be made to do it. Simon loved Jesus too – but from a distance. And then the women, wailing quietly to themselves, stepped forward and gently, so gently, they mopped his face. Jesus thanked them for that – imagine, being in such a state and thanking the women for a service most men would take for granted.

When we arrived at Golgotha, Mary and I stood well back. I didn't want her to see the nailing. She was already broken and desperate. I was worried that she'd do something rash and end up being beaten, and she was showing her years that day.

So Jesus was lifted up. He kept his eyes closed for a while as he concentrated on breathing – it always takes them a while to work out the least painful way to breathe, the least movement in your hands and feet – and then he opened them, as if he knew where we were.

Mary and I, with Salome and Mary Magdalene, were watching, and we knew he could see us. There were many other women as well, but none of the men. They were frightened that they'd be picked up because of their accents. But I speak so little, and because I was with Mary I decided to risk it. What else could I do? Mary was like a mother to me, had been for years. I had to be there with her.

And he died. There was an eclipse, and silence – all the birds stopped singing, and people moved restlessly – seemed like an omen, dark and brooding. He died. He said his last words, and just stopped breathing. He was too exhausted to keep going any longer.

I thought Mary would die too. All those years of wondering and watching, trying to work out the angel, the birth, Joseph's death . . . but she didn't die. In fact, she didn't ever die, but that's another story.

But Jesus did. Joseph of Arimathea was a brave man. He went to ask for the body, and together we laid Jesus to rest, at last. As we placed him in the tomb, Mary wept over him, but with great dignity. I could feel her questions; but for the moment, there were no answers. Just death.

Reflection

You might like just to be quiet and within yourself after this story. Take time to ponder and reflect on the pain and agony.

Thank God that Jesus was prepared to suffer such a cruel death, that we might be redeemed.

34

Mary in the garden

John 20.1–18

It's dark. It's cold. When the sun comes up, the day will warm, but at present it's chill, so you wrap an extra shawl around your shoulders, then set off to the garden.

Peter and John said they wanted to come, but there's no sign of them. Probably still asleep – they didn't sleep Friday night, that's for sure, none of you did. Too scared, lying there, listening for the stamp of the soldiers' boots, the bang on the door, the rough hands dragging you off . . . but it didn't happen. They didn't come. And although you thought they might come last night, at the end of the Sabbath, they didn't, and you slept.

But you knew that you needed to be up early, so you woke up. Always could do that, since you were a child, and went with your mother to get water before the town was awake. You'd trot along behind her, water jar on your shoulder, through the dawn, to the well. She didn't like you going out during the day – people stared, and hissed about you that you were sick, possessed by the devil – but it was worse in the daylight, with people looking, pointing, whispering, or worse. So you learned to be a creature of the dawn and the dusk, when it was safe. You learned to live without others.

This is the path to the garden. Good job you got the herbs last night, and the oils and spices. Gathered up in a pouch, tight, so that people didn't see what you had.

You've come this way before. This is the way you came to hear him, to see him, the first time. You heard the people, talking excitedly about the healer, the prophet, and it grew to such a pitch that you thought, well, why not? Why not go and see? He'll be here in the gloaming, there's such a crowd wanting his touch, his time.

Carefully that time, you snuck along this track, followed along behind until you came to the garden.

And there he was, surrounded by the dregs of Jerusalem: not just the sick, but beggars, prostitutes, tax collectors, and the strangest bunch who were his disciples; they looked like a collection of the throw-outs from other rabbis!

Yes, this is the place; the place where you sat down quietly and listened. You heard him speak. You saw him touch, heal, give hope. You saw the blind receive their sight. You saw the deaf regain their hearing – and heard them shout for joy. You saw the cripples walking. And then he saw you. He saw you despite your careful place at the back. And he saw right into your soul, and called your name.

How did he know your name? How did he know anything – he just did.

And he came over, looked at you, looked into you, and saw it. Saw the years of hiding, of hurt and shame. And he touched you, and it left. You felt it leave, and quietly sobbed your farewell to the spirit that had been your company, your only company, for so long.

So you too became part of that rag, tag and bobtail crew who went in the way. You became special to him; you knew that you were special.

And, at the end, you were there, watching him again, from a distance. Watching through your tears as he bled and died.

And later, you saw where he was laid, in haste, with so little done for him at the last. So you knew, today, that you would come, and do what was required, and what was needed, for him to lie in whatever peace he could find.

Footsteps behind – it's Peter and John. The noise those two make, and as usual, they're trying to outdo each other.

But the light is beginning to come; they'll catch up in a moment.

And so you travel on, down that path . . . arriving at the stone, the stone that should be sealing the tomb, but isn't.

You stare. What's that person doing, over there?

Where is he? Where's Jesus?

Where is Jesus? Where is Jesus, today?

Reflection

Where is Jesus for you, today?

Look for him as you go through the day, and consciously seek him out.

Where is Jesus for you, today?

35

The Ascension

Acts 1.1–14

It's quiet now. You go to your quarters, and lie down, trying to process the day's events. Trying to make sense of what's happened, of what's been happening these last few weeks, last few years.

It all began in the village, the village where you'd lived all your life. Lived with the voices, and known that you were different. Different from the other children, who pointed at you, spat at you, and, if you came too close, pulled your hair and scratched at you. Different from the other young women, shyly carrying water pitchers through the streets to the well, looking at the young men through their eyelashes, trying to spot the one who their parents had spoken of as husband material.

Different from the other women, married with children of their own. Different, because the voices were still there, louder now, and sometimes deafening in their demands.

Until the preacher came. The preacher who spotted you hiding in the street as he went by, and the voices screamed in your head.

Keep away from him! He'll hurt us! Keep away from him – we hate his kind!

And it was as if the preacher could hear the voices. He smiled, so kindly. No one had smiled like that at you since you were a child, a small child, and with his smile the voices started to wail in their fear.

'Leave her alone,' he commanded. And, inside your head, there was quiet. Calm. Peace. Your head was empty of all the voices but your own. And you knew that there was no other way for you but to follow the preacher, come what may.

And it came. Crowds following, listening, questioning, being healed.

And then the other kind of crowd. The one with soldiers, Romans, accusers, Judas.

Betrayal. Death. Anger and shame. Fear and terror.

You remember then the strange words he said at that last meal together: 'This is my body, this is my blood, broken for you, poured out for you . . .'

You heard the words but thought he was losing the plot that night; but now, now you are beginning to understand.

For he who had been dead was now alive. Alive and moving among his friends, alive and speaking to you, breathing and eating, loving and laughing once again.

Until today.

Today he took you for a walk, up the hill of Olivet, where you often went to be together, to pray and talk. When you arrived on the hillside, he began to speak, words that you couldn't comprehend, couldn't fathom – what was that about not knowing times or periods? What was 'the Holy Spirit'? And, most importantly, where has he gone? For go he did, and not in the way that you have almost grown accustomed to over the last few weeks, where he came and went seemingly at will. No, he has gone, and you know that he has gone – period. And then, the men in white robes, as you desperately searched, telling you to go back to Jerusalem and wait . . . wait? Wait for what?

Every time you thought you'd got a handle on life, were beginning to understand, he'd do it again – up-end you in your head and see how long it took you to understand. And he's just gone and done it again – but this time, it feels different. For this time he's gone. And he's not coming back.

Reflection

Think back over a period of your life when God seemed to have withdrawn. How did you cope? Take time to think about the methods that you used to maintain your spiritual life.

Then think about the experience of God seeming to come closer again, and reflect on how that felt.

Thank God that he is always with us, even to the end of the earth.

36

Pentecost

Acts 2

It was like one of those 'before and after' pictures. One minute all was quiet, with everyone watching their backs for fear of the Jews, and the next they were going, well, a bit berserk, really!

Honestly, we were there to wait on table. The eleven, and the others, they were clearly scared rigid, panicking at every sound in case it was the Romans come to take them away too – I know they were better after the events of the first day, the day when they claimed to see Jesus back from the dead, but then they gradually got more and more scared again.

Because he'd gone, hadn't he? And while he seemed to come and go before – when they were talking about seeing him again, and how great it was all going to be – last week they came back from that walk with him, right down and dejected. Someone said that he'd taken them up a hill, and while they were there, they lost him.

Lost him? How do you lose a grown man, I ask? But no, even though he was pretty big, and even though he'd been coming and going, somehow, they said, he'd really gone this time.

And no one has reported seeing him since.

So they carried on meeting together – that was what he'd told them to do, apparently, to carry on meeting together, sharing bread and wine, praying, reading the scriptures. So they carried on. But they were getting more and more nervous, until there we were with the doors locked and everyone jumping like startled sheep.

That day, they'd met early. No one noticed them all gathering in the room – they arrived in dribs and drabs, watching out for who was watching them. They came upstairs, and shared food together. Then there was the sound of the wind getting up – and it was pretty fierce too. The wind blew around the houses, seeming to be circling just round our house. They all looked at each other in amazement. Then there was a crackling sound, and flames started coming down through the ceiling. Yes, I know I sound daft, but honestly, this is just what we saw. The flames spread out, like they had a life of their own, until they sat in the air, hovering just above the eleven and the others – like a private flame each, one that was specially for that particular person.

They still just looked at each other, jaws dropping as the flames slowly melted into their heads . . .

And then it really began! They began to laugh and cry, to slap each other on the back and dance around – like instant intoxication with a touch of hysteria. They laughed and laughed, then they threw the doors open and poured out on to the streets, making so much noise that people just stopped what they were doing and turned round to stare!

And Jerusalem was full of people that day – crowds everywhere – and more and more people came to stare at this seeming bunch of drunks, carousing and cavorting around the square!

Then Peter opened his mouth and began to speak. He spoke to the crowd. He spoke of how God loved them all, and he spoke of Jesus' life and death.

And I realized that this big, hopelessly scared man had become someone completely different. Peter, the oaf, the idiot who always said the wrong thing, had become Peter the preacher, Peter the fisherman who now fishes for people.

I also realized that whatever had happened, no one's life would ever be the same again. And I was right.

Reflection

Has God ever moved in your heart in the way that he moved in Peter's and the other disciples' hearts on the day of Pentecost?

Have you ever witnessed people undergo life changes thanks to the work of God's Spirit?

Pray for people in your church community, for the Spirit of God to sweep through your church and bring changes, so that the kingdom of God might move forward as surely as it did at Pentecost.

37

The raising of Tabitha

Acts 9.36–43

Have you ever been to Joppa? It's part of Tel-Aviv now, part of the great conurbation, but when I lived there, it was a village, by the sea.

I was one of the followers of Jesus. The stories of his life and his death, not to mention his coming back from the dead, reached Joppa quickly, and our little group sprang up. Many of us were poor; I know it's mainly rich people who follow the way now, but in those days, the slaves and servants were the Christians. We found dignity, and worth, through following the way. Here was someone who told us that God loved us, despite our position in life; that we were important to God, if not to our masters and lords. A faith, a religion, that said I was recognized by God. I'd never heard anything like it before, or since.

And Tabitha, or Dorcas in Greek, she was one of our number.

Tabitha was a follower before me. I met her when I became a widow, and she heard that I was left with nothing. She took me into her home, and clothed me with some of the wonderful garments that she wove herself. And so I met the other followers and joined the way. I was baptized one spring morning, by the edge of the great sea. Tabitha became my friend, and while staying at her house, I became part of an ever-growing number of people that she sought out and helped, who nearly all became followers. We all saw the change it had made in other people's lives.

We met week by week to share bread and wine, to talk and to pray, and Tabitha was one of the key people of the group. So that was different too – a faith that allowed women to speak, to pray? Now that was new! Mind you, it didn't last for long – once people realized we were threatening the social order, we women found ourselves being silenced by the men who ran the show. But that's another story.

It began early one morning.

Tabitha was unwell, running a fever and with pain in her head. She couldn't get out of bed, so we helped all we could, drawing the water from the well, cleaning and cooking together. As the day went by, and it got hotter and hotter, so Tabitha sank into a fever from which she was not to awaken.

We sponged her down as her temperature rose further, and she tossed and turned on her bed. We took it in turns to sit with her through the night, doing what we could. We arranged for the group to pray without cease, that God would not call her home; Tabitha was a magnet for the cause, helping so many, loved by us all.

But it was not to be. She died early in the morning, quietly, without a fuss. She just breathed her last, and began to go cold.

We sat with the body for a while, then we went to buy the spices to love her in the last way we could. As we were washing her and preparing her for the ground, we heard that Peter was on his way! The big fisherman! Coming here, to help us? We had heard about his miraculous ways. We had heard him speaking, years before, of his life with the Lord; of his own mistakes, and how the Lord always drew him through his mistakes, forgiving and loving.

So we wept and waited. Waited and wept. Could he? Would he? More importantly, would God?

He eventually arrived as evening fell. I had forgotten his size – he really had been a working fisherman, his shoulders told you that. And he was like us; not smart, not rich, just a follower of the Lord, walking in the way with us. He carried with him an aura of calm, of peace and certainty. If anyone could help us, Peter could.

He sent us all out of the room, and shut the door. Tabitha told me, later, that she just heard him call her name, just as he had heard Jesus call Jairus' daughter all those years ago: 'Tabitha, come.'

She came. She won't talk about where she was while her body was growing cold, what she saw and heard; but when she tells the tale, a faraway look enters her eyes, and then she'll smile and go quiet.

She woke up, as from a sleep, sat up and rubbed her eyes like a small child. She said that Peter smiled at her – the rich smile of total accepting love – and then looked amazed himself at what had happened, as she got up out of the bed, and came through to greet us.

So she carried on, being there for people in need, helping the church as we grew, helping people whom I shall never meet.

Her healing became the talk of the town. But she never joined with that talk. She would simply say, 'Here I am. God clearly wasn't ready for me yet.'

So I count each day with her a blessing, and praise the God who can heal, even death, giving new life for those who have fallen into sin, and hatred and despair.

For while Tabitha seemed to be the one who was healed that day, later we realized that many of us were healed too, given new life and new faith through what took place.

I have never seen anyone come back from the dead since. I doubt if you have. But the healing of God's spirit, I'm told, continues even in your day. Even in your life – you just have to ask, and wait.

Reflection

Few people, if any, have witnessed this sort of revival of the dead. But God continues to heal in different ways. Where do you need healing in your life? Which part of you is dead, and lost?

Prayer

Lord heal me, deep within.
Reach down to my deadness and bring new life.
Reach down within my heart and bring new hope.
Reach down within my soul, and revive and restore.
Lord, heal me, deep within.
Amen.

38

A letter from Thessalonica

1 Thessalonians 1

Dear Silas,

Thank you for your letter. I can't believe how long it is now since we sent that first letter to the saints in Thessalonica, or how wonderfully God has supplied their needs and filled their hearts with his Spirit. The church there is such a treasure.

Do you remember how we first went there? The peculiar vision that Paul had that night, of the Macedonian man pleading with him to 'come and help us'. Paul certainly believed the call was of the Lord – how we changed direction and headed off that way! I think that was the first time I met Luke – though I'd heard his name before. What a blessing Luke was to all of us, but to Paul in particular.

It was such a strange few weeks, wasn't it? Arriving in Philippi, where Paul and yourself were fallen upon by that crowd after sharing the gospel, and had to spend the night in prison. Do you remember the governor's face when he realized you were Roman citizens? Laugh – I would have laughed out loud if they hadn't given you such a battering. Wow, but he was scared for his own skin; he really begged us to leave, didn't he? So we did, and travelled on to Thessalonica.

What a lovely place, with that beautiful synagogue: good Jewish population, and those lovely women who attended the synagogue, despite being gentiles, drawn by the truth of what they heard and saw there.

I don't remember anywhere else where the Spirit had so gone before us, preparing the hearts of the people for the gospel. They were so quickly convinced that Jesus was the Messiah – and the hospitality! Jason and Aristarchus were the best hosts . . . even the pagans converted. Must be something about the gentle life they lead there, the respect for different faiths, that meant that they recognized the truth when they heard it.

But then there was the riot – do you remember how Paul referred to the 'rent-a-mob'; 'certain lewd fellows of the baser sort' – I'll say. They wanted us out – and out Paul went. How it broke his heart, as that autumn he was forced to travel first to Athens and then to Corinth. He was a quivering wreck when he got there – thank the Lord that Priscilla and Aquila were there and could care for him.

I remember being so depressed when we first wrote to the Thessalonians – we had to leave them only a few weeks after we had first met them, and it felt that surely that little gathering would not survive. How God likes to surprise us!

But I went back a short while ago, and I found a wonderful fellowship of Christians who were steadfast in their faith and witness, despite the persecution. They still spoke of our second visit, five years after the first, and do you know, they had kept that first letter we wrote. They say that it's the first letter that Paul wrote, and they're keeping it; they still get it out and share it at meetings. It was sent just 20 years after our Lord ascended . . . and now it's so many more.

Take heart, Silas; the church in Thessalonica is alive and well. Their love is spoken of, and converts more to the faith than any words could do. The Lord is seen in all that they do: peaceful, kind and open-hearted people one and all.

How I wish that more fellowships were as open to the work of the Spirit as those folk in Thessalonica.

Can we meet soon? I too have had news of the church in Jerusalem, and would like to share it with you. Perhaps we could meet at Corinth soon. I'll wait for you here.

May God's love fill you with his peace and joy as we wait for the Lord to come.

Timothy

Reflection

Think back over the years that you have been worshipping at your present church. Think what it was like when you joined, and compare that with what it is like now.

Has it grown and changed? Or has it gone backwards, becoming more closed and less inclusive?

Pray for your local church community, that it might grow and change as surely as the church at Thessalonica.

39

From Andrew

Matthew 4.12–23

Dear Matthew,

I was interested when you wrote asking me for my remembrances of my time with the Lord. The story has been so well told in the fellowship, that I somehow never expected it to be committed to scroll. But you are right, we are getting older, we are becoming forgetful, and you do need to catch the tale before it is lost to our children's children.

It was many years ago that I met the Lord, but I remember it as if he were here today. I had been by the Jordan, listening to the Baptist, and trying to work out who he was. John always said that he was the voice of one crying in the wilderness, not the chosen one, but his voice was powerful and his message strong. I was baptized by John, as was Simon and many, many others, and we spent hours by the river listening and learning, and, in some strange way, waiting.

Waiting for the Messiah.

Ah! We were all waiting in those days. The Roman occupation sat heavily on our shoulders; how we longed for King David to come and drive them out, restoring to us the Land of our Fathers, promised to us by Moses and Joshua, by the prophets and by all that we learned at Rabbinic school when we were boys.

So we waited.

I don't remember the day exactly, but the sun was just coming out after a cloudburst. A man, whom John clearly knew, came down to the Jordan to be baptized. John refused – and at that we all took note – John refusing to baptize someone! Now this was odd!

There was an exchange, with John saying that this man should baptize *him*. But then he was persuaded to do it for the stranger.

What was even stranger was that as the man came up out of the water, there was a rumble, like thunder – yet the sun came out, on his head as he stood, wet, in the river. The thunder sounded more like a deep, deep voice, and the crowd murmured together, scared and wondering what was happening.

And then he turned around and walked away, towards the wilderness, and he was gone.

John said that his name was Jesus, and that he was John's cousin, on his mother's side.

It was after this, soon after this, that John was arrested, and we went home to Galilee, back to our fishing and our families.

Some time later, we were by the sea at Capernaum, where we worked. We were out working, throwing the nets and pulling them in. It was a good day for it, and we were thinking about finishing and going home, when we saw Jesus in the distance. He came up to us, and without a by your leave, an introduction or anything as straightforward as that, he said to us:

'Follow me, and I will make you fish for people.'

He made it sound like a huge adventure, as if it was the most obvious thing in the world.

We looked at each other, not quite sure how to react. Then Simon, huge, strong Simon, sort of glazed over. He put down the net, and walked off, after Jesus. So I put down my end, and went too. We walked down the shore, to where James and John were mending their nets, and they followed too. Zebedee didn't seem to mind at all – he just called out that he'd pack up and take our kit home to Simon's. And the four of us walked off, into a different life.

What did we do? Too much to write down. We did very little other than watch, and learn, and listen. He didn't make a show of anything that he did, though; he quietly went about, healing people who had been sick for ever, or just a short while. He touched the possessed and they were delivered, he talked with the unclean, he touched the untouchables. He gave sight to the blind, hearing to the deaf, and freedom to those who were imprisoned by bars either of others' prejudice, or of their own making. He changed my life.

And in time, I did catch people. I too was able to share my experience of the Lord, and it helped others to know that he is still alive, still active, still calling others to catch yet more people.

And I shall continue to cast my nets for the rest of my life, for that is what he called me to do.

And you, Matthew? How will you catch folks? Through this great scroll of yours? I pray that the Spirit will indeed give his life to your words as you write them, that all who hear them, down through the centuries, will hear how our Lord chose to call insignificant people such as myself and Peter, and transform all that we were into something I would never have believed.

May all who hear truly have ears to hear, and the openness of the heart that can lead to the kingdom coming.

Every blessing on you, from myself, and Simon.

Andrew

Reflection

Do you have many Christian friends who are nearing the end of their natural life? Have you talked with them about their journey of faith?

Find out as much as you can from the older members of your faith community about their Christian lives. Perhaps put together a record of their stories, and be encouraged by what God has done for them.

40

A bishop's tale

Philemon

Philemon has at least got a good sense of humour – or maybe it's irony. When I was born he named me Onesimus, which means 'useful'.

My family were slaves in Philemon's household in Colossi, and I remember the first time Paul came. He spoke in the market place, and Philemon heard him. He invited Paul to come and speak at our house in town, and later stayed in the villa just outside the town. I loved Paul when I was a child – he seemed to care for us, the slaves, in a different way; we were nothings to most people. True, we had our friends and family within the slave community, but the free people, they never spoke to us unless it was to tell us what to do, or how we'd done something wrong, again.

Paul spoke to us like we speak to each other. I never forgot that.

So, when Philemon sent me to Rome, many years later, with a letter for Paul, and some money, food and clothes, now that he was under house arrest, I was thrilled. I remember hugging myself in anticipation of all that would happen, on the journey, and then in Rome itself. I'd never been to Rome, and for the master to send me was a high compliment. It meant he trusted me.

What a fool he was! There was I, 16 years old, let loose after a life of slavery! Not really let loose – anyone could see I was a slave on a journey for the master – but to be out of Colossi, travelling to the city of Rome, just with the others from Philemon's house . . . imagine what I could get up to!

So, we got there, took in the sights – and the smells! – and did what we'd been sent to do. Then it was time to go back, and I began to get my doubts. Why should I go back to being only slightly better than the cattle, and treated worse that the master's favourite horse? Why shouldn't I stay here and work for Paul, who really appreciated me, and helped me to see myself in a new light – for he still spoke to me, befriended me, seemed to think that I was worth more for myself than what I was – a piece of property. And someone else's property at that.

So, the day the others left, I went AWOL. They just didn't know where I was, and eventually went down to the docks without me to catch the ship back . . .

Paul found me later that day, skulking in his kitchen with Esther, his housekeeper. He immediately realized what I'd done, and that I'd now committed a capital crime. After a while thinking, he decided to keep me, and see how it went. The next boat didn't sail for a week, after all . . .

But what I hadn't realized was that Paul was still a Christian. I'd forgotten that he'd been preaching the faith when he stayed before – how I managed to overlook that is beyond me now, but, I was young and impetuous once . . . He lived a life of such holiness, but accessible holiness, that I quite came under the spell. It wasn't long before I was listening to him preach, and joining him at prayer; and after that first week, I was recognizing that my childhood baptism at Philemon's house now meant something. Not only did I come from a Christian household, I was a Christian myself.

Time passed. Not that much, perhaps a few weeks, before Paul summoned me one day. He told me that I couldn't stay, that I had to return to my rightful master.

I was terrified – Philemon could kill me for what I'd done, and he was a man of short temper. He'd trusted me, and I'd betrayed that trust . . .

Paul grabbed my arm as I went to run. And he explained what he proposed to do. He had written a letter, explaining everything, and asking Philemon, as Paul's friend, to forgive me, one Christian to another. To restore me to the household, even possibly to free me . . . And I was to deliver the letter myself.

I took some persuading. I was not convinced that this seemingly hopeless letter idea would work . . . but Paul said that we had to do it, it was the right thing to do.

So that is what I did.

Later that week, I boarded the next ship for Greece, and then travelled on to Colossi. Guards came and put me in chains, and I was taken before the master. When he saw that I'd brought a letter he was clearly surprised, and when he read it he was amazed.

'Forgive you? A runaway slave? What sort of example is the man asking me to set? All my slaves will run away next!'

I said nothing; just prayed and waited. Then he laughed aloud, and shouted, 'OK then! You win, Paul! I'll do it!'

I wasn't freed then, but many years later, when Philemon died. All his slaves were given freedom if they wanted it – and not everyone did.

But I took the freedom that had been bought so dearly by Paul. For Paul had been executed a year after I left him.

Me, I became a monk, a travelling preacher. Eventually I became a presbyter of the local church, and then later I was called to Ephesus, where today I write my memoirs. I'm the bishop now . . . who'd have believed it? As Paul said in that letter, which I still have, indeed, I've lived up to that once ironic name. God has found me useful, even if it didn't seem as if I would be of any use to anyone at one time. And I expect God will continue to use me, perhaps even through these writings . . .

Reflection

God took a somewhat diffident slave, and transformed him to become a bishop of the early church.

Imagine what God could do for you!

Prayer

Lord God, we thank you for the amazing way that you lead us, your people.
When we are bogged down in the detail, help us to see the bigger picture.
When we are blind to the bigger picture, help us to know that you do care, and that you do lead us on.
Amen.